S0-BYS-730

The Provincial Universities of Mexico

Richard G. King
with
Alfonso Rangel Guerra
David Kline
Noel F. McGinn

A cooperative project of the International Council for Educational Development, New York; Asociación Nacional de Universidades e Institutos de Enseñanza Superior, Mexico City; and Center for Studies in Education and Development, Harvard University.

The Provincial Universities of Mexico

An Analysis of Growth and Development

Praeger Publishers New York Washington London

PRAEGER SPECIAL STUDIES IN INTERNATIONAL ECONOMICS AND DEVELOPMENT

PRAEGER PUBLISHERS
111 Fourth Avenue, New York, N.Y. 10003, U.S.A.
5, Cromwell Place, London S.W.7, England

Published in the United States of America in 1971
by Praeger Publishers, Inc.

Library of Congress Catalog Card Number: 74-163928

Printed in the United States of America

PREFACE

This book, the product of a unique intellectual partnership between Mexican and North American scholars, should be especially useful to three quite different audiences: those interested in Latin American education and development; those throughout the world concerned with strengthening educational planning and management, particularly in higher education; and a smaller group of specialists with a technical interest in analytical methodologies.

The study makes notable contributions on all three scores. By shedding revealing light on nine rapidly growing and increasingly important provincial universities in Mexico, it helps indirectly to illuminate the comparable problems, potentials, and dynamics of many other Latin American institutions. Beyond this, it demonstrates a novel methodology for getting at some of the qualitative aspects of educational assessment and planning that are of universal concern.

Today, these qualitative aspects are on the frontier of crucial issues confronting theory and practice in educational planning and management. Impressive advances were made during the 1960s in evolving and applying new quantitative planning concepts and techniques of educational planning. These advances dealt, for example, with the projection of youth populations, the setting of enrollment targets, and the "costing" of these targets in terms of the classrooms, teachers, and money required to achieve them. Significant progress also was made toward integrating educational planning with economic planning, particularly through the medium of manpower planning.

All this has been helpful--up to a point. But it has become increasingly clear that a mechanistic brand of quantitative planning that focuses on the outer parameters of educational systems and institutions and takes their internal arrangements and premises for granted fails to come to grips with the hardest challenges now facing education. Indeed, this sort of planning, unrelieved by major qualitative considerations, can sometimes do more harm than good by giving a false illusion of progress and by concealing imperative needs for educational change.

This seems to have been the case in at least some of the many instances in recent years where quantitative planning has been handmaiden to a narrow educational strategy aimed primarily at accelerating the expansion of enrollments with little or no provision for adapting educational structures, curriculum, and methods to fit changes in the social-economic-technological environment or in the needs and characteristics of the student clientele. Such a strategy has in many places been rewarded by striking success--statistically. But behind the statistical facade one finds abundant evidence that these enormously expanded educational systems have now ended in the throes of a profound and worsening crisis--a crisis of painful maladjustment between unchanging educational institutions and their rapidly changing environment.

Clearly, what is now called for, not simply in Mexico but throughout the world, is an educational strategy combining selective growth with change and innovation that will keep the internal affairs and practices of educational institutions in tune with their changing times and local circumstances. Such a strategy will call for a more sophisticated and realistic kind of educational planning that pierces the outer envelope of macro-planning and comes directly to grips with redesigning the various subsystems and internal processes of the overall educational system, employing the concepts and principles of systems analysis. In short, educational planning needs to become the inspirer and promoter of educational innovation and change, not the enlarger and perpetuator of the educational *status quo*.

This sort of "planning for change" that deals with the qualitative features as well as the quantitative ones will not be easy, but it will be a great deal more dynamic, creative, and challenging than simple linear planning. Moreover, it offers the only real hope for escaping from the educational crisis. To get very far with it, however, any educational system or institution will need to begin by heeding the old exhortation: Know thyself! For example, before any university can plot a sensible future path of self-development, it must first gain a clear understanding of where it has recently been, where it stands now, how well or poorly it is presently performing and the reasons why, where it is trending, and what leeway and options it has for shaping its own future evolution and performance.

It is precisely here that the present study makes a useful contribution. In examining the nine provincial Mexican universities, the study reaches beyond the customary quantitative indicators and seeks to identify and assess some of the critical qualitative factors that seriously influence each institution's behavior, caliber, and direction of movement. This pioneering effort will need further work and trial, but it is an imaginative and promising start in an important fresh direction.

Some readers who could profit considerably from this book may be put off too quickly by the rather formidable-looking analytical methods discussed in certain sections. In our view, they can afford to skip lightly over these sticky portions and still be well rewarded by reading the less technical portions that constitute the bulk of the book.

The Advisory Group on United States-Mexican Educational Relations that produced this study was formed in the mid-1960s through the initiative of Education and World Affairs, a predecessor of the International Council for Educational Development (established in late 1970). This is the final study in a series of useful studies produced by this Advisory Group.*

Although it is not feasible to call the full roll of the many individuals--above and below the Rio Grande--who contributed to the present publication, we must give credit to those people who played especially important roles: to Russell G. Davis, Chairman of the Committee on United States-Mexican Educational Relations and to two of the Committee's members, Victor L. Urquidi, President of El Colegio de México, and Alfonso Rangel Guerra, Secretary General of Mexico's National Association of Universities and Institutes of Higher Education, who were responsible for initiating this study; to Richard G. King, then lecturer on education and research associate at Harvard's Center for Studies in Education and Development, who with Mr. Rangel jointly directed the study. Mr. King prepared the text and Appendix material; Mr. Rangel is the author of the concluding chapter. To them, to David Kline and Noel F. McGinn, who made important contributions to the statistical methodology and interpretation, and to all their colleagues in this cooperative international venture, we extend the sincere thanks and congratulations of Education and World Affairs and its successor organization.

Philip H. Coombs
Vice Chairman
International Council for
Educational Development

---

*Blanca M. de Petricioli and Clark Winton Reynolds, The Teaching of Economics in Mexico, 1967.

Russell G. Davis, Scientific, Engineering and Technical Education in Mexico, 1967.

Charles Nash Myers, U.S. University Activity Abroad: Implications of the Mexican Case, 1968.

Noel F. McGinn with Russell G. Davis and Richard G. King, The Technology of Instruction in Mexican Universities, 1969.

ACKNOWLEDGMENTS

This venture in cooperative research comes about as a result of a series of discussions held by the Committee on United States-Mexican Educational Relations of Education and World Affairs (now the International Council for Educational Development) during 1967. As noted in the Preface, the principal supporters of the enterprise were the Committee Chairman, Russell G. Davis, who is Professor of Education at Harvard University, and two of the Committee's members, Victor L. Urquidi, President of El Colegio de México, and Alfonso Rangel Guerra, Secretary General of Mexico's National Association of Universities and Institutes of Higher Education.

Professor Davis and President Urquidi were particularly helpful during the planning stages, as were EWA staff members Charles N. Myers and Joel Johnson. Lic. Rangel and members of his Association's staff shared the task of designing the study and its questionnaires and undertook the thankless job of collecting all the data. Coding of the questionnaire material was accomplished in Cambridge, Mass., with the invaluable assistance of Susana Bernard and Mary Lesser. Organization of the data for machine processing and actual computer programming were expertly handled by Elizabeth Truesdell with the assistance of Joanne Dahlgren. Lic. Rangel provided advice, logistical support, and interpretation throughout the course of the study and is the author of its concluding chapter. David Kline provided major assistance in planning the computer analysis, while Noel F. McGinn participated both in the computer analysis and in the organization and several revisions of the presentation of the study. Hans Simons offered valuable criticism of the text. Mary Louise King assisted with the first editorial corrections. Responsibility for any errors of fact or analysis in the text and in the appendixes is, nevertheless, mine.

Direct financial assistance for the study came from Education and World Affairs, and indirect subsidy came from the Ford Foundation through its support of the research activities of the Center for Studies in Education and Development, Harvard University.

But our greatest indebtedness is to the rectors, deans, and professors of the nine universities who gave so unselfishly of their time to offer thoughtful answers to the questions presented to them. If the ordering and analysis of their responses contributes in any way to the improvement of the profession of university teaching in Mexico, the study will have been worthwhile.

Richard G. King

CONTENTS

Chapter | Page

Chapter | Page

LIST OF TABLES

LIST OF APPENDIX TABLES

Appendix
Table | Page

Appendix Table		Page

Appendix
Table | Page

INTRODUCTION: AIMS OF THE STUDY

In the 1960s, greatly improved information about students, professors, and programs in the universities of Latin America became available through the various international agencies and particularly through the secretariats of voluntary associations of universities at the regional and national level. The present study, organized by one of the latter, the Asociación de Universidades e Institutos de Enseñanza Superior (ANUIES), describes and analyzes an important segment of higher education in Mexico. It is appropriate that ANUIES has chosen to focus its attention on the provincial universities, for they have received all too little attention in comparison with the older, larger, better-known, better-supported institutions of Mexico's Federal District, the area that includes and surrounds Mexico City.

The provincial university is "provincial" not because it is narrow or simple but because it is in the provinces--that is to say, in one of the states outside Mexico's Federal District. The growth of higher education in Mexico has been very much a federal enterprise and the role of the states has been relatively minor until very recently. For sheer demographic reasons if for no others, this role must become much more important. The provincial university must grow, must respond to the changing needs of its region, and must develop a higher potential for effective instruction if rapidly increasing regional populations are to be served adequately.

This study seeks to provide ANUIES and its newly formed National Center for the Planning of Higher Education with relevant information about the qualitative and quantitative characteristics of the institutions outside the Federal District, which must bear the heaviest burden of providing higher education to Mexico's soaring school population. The emphasis in the study is on those institutional characteristics that are most relevant to the new social and economic demands of the region. The methodology is both to establish comparative norms and to analyze statistically inter-relationships of the variables designed to measure responsiveness and instructional potential, as well as quantitative output. Our hope is that the analysis will prove useful in suggesting the areas that most need attention in the proximate future.

Much or most of what is described will be of no surprise to Mexican university professors and administrators; however, much will surprise those whose views of all Latin American universities are colored by certain negative stereotypes that have appeared in the literature on higher education in Latin America. These stereotypes suggest that the Latin American university is elitist; unconcerned with the social and economic problems of the society; dedicated to perpetuating a small professional "establishment" composed of isolated, uncooperative professional faculties and emphasizing clinical instruction for the practice of an outdated profession; unresponsive to changes in technology; archaic in instructional methodology; cumbersome and ineffective in administration; and, worst of all, dependent on a teaching faculty of disinterested, uncommitted, out-of-date, full-time practitioners who "also teach" at the university. Hopefully, for those whose opinions are less wedded to these stereotypical extremes the study will be informative in its ordering and analysis of the facts and opinions derived from a survey of directors, deans, and professors.

Certain disclaimers in regard to the methodology of the study should be made at the outset. This is not a manpower study, although a manpower economist might well be interested in some of the characteristics of institutions of higher education that seem to facilitate or to block the preparation of the numbers and kinds of specialists he feels the provincial regions may need for development. This study is neither a sociological analysis nor an attempt to develop a theory of development through examination of the interface between university and society, although sociologists of various schools may find in this small volume facts to support or disprove their theories. Nor is this primarily an attempt to apply psychometrics, linear programming, and other systematic methods to educational data in the name of educational planning, although we have used several multivariate techniques to aid in our description. The study is neither sociology nor history nor economics.

Instead, it is an attempt to organize systematically some pertinent information about higher education in "provincial" Mexico. Its purpose is descriptive and not prescriptive. The general shape and content of the questionnaires have necessarily determined the general form and content of the results; the particular observations, the specific examples, the suggestions, and the criticisms are entirely those of the respondents. The study is prompted by the curiosity of the administrator rather than that of the social scientist. Perhaps its identification is more with educational administration than with social science and its thrust merely empirical rather than scientific. Sometimes, the mere ordering of facts (empiricism) must precede the formulation of theory (science).

CHAPTER 1
HERITAGE AND GROWTH

The provincial universities of Mexico, born out of the Mexican Revolution of the twentieth century, are a breed apart from the prototypical Latin American university of this and earlier eras. Yet the structure, the philosophy, the customs, and even the procedures of the provincial university reflect to an important extent the four-century heritage of the colonial and Napoleonic universities. An awareness of that earlier historical heritage and a comparative look at more recent statistics on higher education in Latin America should help us to understand the relatively recent history of the institutions we are about to study. In this chapter, therefore, we sketch a brief historical and comparative background preparatory to a discussion of the growth and financing of the provincial universities.

HISTORICAL CONTEXT

The separate historical streams that led to the founding of the North American and Latin American colonial universities have been described frequently. Bologna, the progenitor of the southern European universities, was founded in the twelfth century by unions of students from trans-Alpine Europe anxious to study civil as well as canon law. Paris, the parent of the English universities, was an outgrowth of the cathedral schools, a center for theological studies organized by its professors under the Bishop of Paris. Bologna's influence in passing through Salamanca received the further impetus of the medieval liberal arts and sciences (the trivium and the quadrivium) but led in the New World to a theological university founded by religious orders with the joint approval of the Pope and the King of Spain and chartered by the Council of the Indies. On the other hand, the theology of Paris became the philosophy and letters of the Renaissance and then the Reformation in Oxford and Cambridge and, in privately funded, anti-Establishment, sectarian colleges in the New World, the humanistic studies necessary to the general preparation, first of Protestant ministers and later of other professionals. In the northern New World, the study of arts and sciences at the university level thus became preparatory to professional studies, while in the southern New World, arts and sciences (or philosophy and letters) became and remained an alternative to the professional studies, which in the three "colonial" centuries were theology, law, and medicine.

The eighteen institutions in the southern New World flowered earlier and reached their first full bloom sometime before the expulsion of the Jesuits from the colonies by King Charles III of Spain in 1767. The northern New World universities acquired distinction a century later as natural science was introduced into the undergraduate curriculum, as land grant colleges were founded to provide instruction in the mechanical arts and applied sciences, and as the research graduate school was imported from Germany.

Latin America was wracked by revolution in the early nineteenth century. The Bourbon King of Spain was opposed by the New World elites, but the revolution did not fundamentally change the lot of the common man. Independence of the Old World state carried with it a degree of separation from the Church. In the new republics, the old theological universities became loose collections of professional schools designed, like the Napoleonic university, to provide the state with groups of professionals and, incidentally, to perpetuate a _criollo_ elite in the New World. During the ensuing century, such new professional faculties as engineering, economics, and pharmacy were added, but in general they were neither integrated nor coordinated with existing faculties. The explicit function of higher education was professional training for clearly defined vocational specialties.

As governments were overturned by military coups during the century from 1820 to 1920 and as forces within the university expressed dissatisfaction with governments in power, the university was frequently invaded by police or the military and student lives were lost. Only in the light of this heritage of violence can one understand the post-1918 reform movement with its rigid insistence on an apparently absolutistic autonomy--even isolation--from agencies of the state and what seemed an unnecessarily politicized system of internal government. Although the present confrontation of national guardsmen or police and students in U.S. universities is but a pale copy of the confrontations during the past century in Latin American universities, it does suggest for the first time to citizens of the United States what can happen when government policy produces moral outrage in the universities or, conversely, when political action in the universities produces exasperation in government.

The modern university reform movement began at the University of Córdoba in Argentina in 1918. In its attempt to provide freedom from state interference in the institution as a whole and freedom of expression to professors, the reform was revolutionary. The institution or reinstitution of _cogobierno_ (participation of students in university government) was, in a sense, less revolutionary and more a return to tradition. In any case, the package was widely appealing, particularly if one accepted as a postulate that the university inevitably must be opposed to the government in power. The reform movement swept all of Spanish-speaking America, although its history in Mexico, which was then in the process of a real people's revolution (that is, a revolution in which the common people gain control of the government), was somewhat different, since government participation in administrative appointments and in arrangements for special research and training was--and still is--accepted.

It is not our purpose here to speculate about the historical consequences of university autonomy for national social and economic development. Judged in terms of numbers of universities and numbers of students, higher education in Latin America (with the exception of Argentina) was not in a position to play a major role in those aspects of national life in the nineteenth and early twentieth centuries. Precisely because of the universities' autonomy, it is difficult to get historical estimates of enrollments from government sources, and it is only since World War II that the universities themselves--through voluntary associations like the Unión de Universidades de América Latina and Mexico's Asociación Nacional de Universidades e Institutos de Enseñanza Superior (ANUIES) or the international agencies like UNESCO, the Organization of American States, or the Inter-American Development Bank--have collected statistics that permit international and intranational comparisons.[1]

GROWTH OF UNIVERSITIES IN LATIN AMERICA

Although the first universities in the New World were founded in the middle of the sixteenth century (at Santo Domingo in 1538 and at Mexico and Lima in 1551), only 9 more universities had been founded by 1700 and only 6 more were founded during the eighteenth century. This total was a bit more than doubled during the post-revolutionary period of the nineteenth century. Although a few universities passed out of existence or into suspended animation at that time, the opening of the twentieth century saw fewer than 40 operating universities in all of Latin America, about the same number of full-fledged universities as there are in Mexico today (33). (The definition of a university in 1900, as now, is not always clear, but in general it means an institution of higher education having at least two professional faculties linked by some central organization.) By 1950, 105 universities were operating in Latin America and by 1967 there were 228, although the total of all institutions of higher education was about 1,000.[2] By comparison, Mexico had only one real university in 1910;[3] 7 by 1940; 12 by 1950; and 33 by 1967, with a grand total of 103 institutions of higher education in 1967.[4] So the rate of founding of new universities since World War II in Mexico exceeds even the remarkably rapid rate for Latin America as a whole.

An idea of the relative age of types of faculties in Mexican universities generally and in the nine universities being studied can be gained from Appendix Table 1. The median age (nearly 100 years) of law school faculties is explained by the number of independent law schools operating in the nineteenth century. These, together with the _colegios civiles_ and the state _institutos_, were the forerunners of the twentieth-century state universities. The median age of all other faculties in the nine universities, however, is less than 20 years.

The importance of the relative youth of the universities being studied and the relative youth of their professors, deans, and rectors will become apparent in the study and will help to explain why a number of the earlier stereotypes of the Latin American university and its teaching faculty do not seem to hold for Mexico. Institutional practices in an old university are more likely to reflect old customs and habits than are practices in a new university.

The rapid increase in the number of Latin American universities is reflected in a rapidly rising student enrollment. Annual estimates of university enrollments for all of Latin America prior to World War II are generally not available. The total enrollment for 1955 was about 380,000; in 1960 it was about 510,000; and in 1966 it was estimated at 880,000, a growth rate of 6.5 percent per year in the period 1955-60 and 9.5 percent per year during 1960-66.[5] In Mexico, the number of students registered in higher education is estimated to have been about 25,000 in 1940; 79,000 in 1960; and 132,000 in 1966,[6] a closely comparable rate of growth.

Mexico's total of 132,000 registered students at the professional level in 1966 placed it third in total enrollment in Latin America, behind Argentina (256,000) and Brazil (158,000). The giant National Autonomous University of Mexico (Universidad Nacional Autónoma de México or UNAM), with 45,000 students at the professional level, was second only to the University of Buenos Aires with 93,000; these two institutions alone enrolled over one-sixth of all university students in Latin America in 1966.[7] According to ANUIES, total enrollments at the professional level in Mexico for 1967 were 154,000, with 84,000 of these in the Federal District.[8] Of the latter, 48,000 were in the UNAM, which had already introduced a policy of restricted admissions for candidates outside the Federal District.

Mexico's students distribute themselves among the several professional _carreras_ (programs) in a fashion somewhat different from that of Latin American universities as a whole, as shown in Table 1. Of note in Mexico are the relatively high figures for engineering and business administration and the relatively low figures for law, humanities, education, and miscellaneous _carreras_. There has been an obvious concentration on "development-related" _carreras_. One wonders, however, whether the training of secondary-level teachers is being slighted, since the total for humanities, education, and miscellaneous _carreras_ includes the enrollments of the higher normal schools. No doubt the newer faculties of natural sciences are good training grounds for prospective teachers of science. It is less likely that a business or law school is the best source of preparation for a teacher of social sciences and humanities.

Table 1

Distribution of Students by _Carrera_ in Mexico and Latin America, 1967

Carrera	Mexico		Latin America	
	Thousands of Students	Percent of Total	Thousands of Students	Percent of Total
Medical and dental sciences	25.0	17	140	17
Natural sciences	7.5	5	27	3
Engineering and architecture	40.0	27	133	16
Agronomy and veterinary medicine	2.5	2	30	4
Business administration and economics	45.0	30	142	17
Law and social sciences	19.0	12	169	20
Philosophy, humanities, and other	11.0	7	189	23
Total	150.0	100	830	100

Source: Social Progress Trust Fund, _Socio-Economic Progress in Latin America_ (Washington, D.C.: Inter-American Development Bank, 1968).

Although Mexico ranks high among Latin American countries in terms of total number of enrolled university students, its standing in terms of enrollment as a percentage of the population of university age is more modest. In 1966, the relationship between total university enrollment and the total population in the 20-to-24-year age group, expressed as a percentage, was 4.4 for Latin America as a whole, but ranged from 14.1 in Argentina to 1.4 in Honduras. In Mexico, the percentage was 3.8.[9] (Admittedly, Mexico's demographic pyramid is flatter than that of Argentina because of a much higher rate of population growth.)

Thus, despite an extremely high rate of growth in higher education in recent years, Mexico's international position is not yet impressive. Furthermore, the overall national percentage of university-age population attending a university fails to indicate the wide variation of attendance among regions within Mexico. Charles N. Myers has pointed out that Mexico's educational development, like its economic development, has brought its Federal District to the level of the most developed areas of the world but has left some of its rural areas, particularly in the south, at the level of some of the least developed parts of the world.[10] Thus, in 1960, at a time when the national percentage of university enrollment to population aged 20 to 24 was 2.7, the comparable percentage in the Federal District was 12.9. The corresponding national and Federal District figures in 1940 were 1.3 and 8.3, while in the rapidly industrializing state of Nuevo León, the percentage was 1.6 in 1940 and rose to 7.3 in 1960.[11] Since over half the enrollment in higher education is in the Federal District, it easily can be inferred that higher education in most of Mexico outside its few largest cities (Mexico, Monterrey, and Guadalajara) is quantitatively comparable to that of the least developed countries of Latin America.

GROWTH OF UNIVERSITIES IN MEXICO

It is easy to forget how relatively recent is Mexico's surge toward mass education. National efforts to provide rural education began only after José Vasconcelos, then Rector of the National University, designed and organized the new Ministry of Education in 1920. Vasconcelos' vision of the rural school, his casa del pueblo, however conservative in terms of its academic content, was revolutionary in terms of its intent to redistribute federal benefits to the periphery. Vasconcelos' work, the work of his pedagogically more progressive lieutenants, Moisés Saenz and Rafael Ramirez, in the 1920s, and that of the more socialistic Narcisso Bassols in the early 1930s was capped by Lázaro Cárdenas' rural, social, and economic reforms in the late 1930s and his forceful execution of a national program of land reform.[12] Population growth, which was actually negative during the early bloody years of the Mexican Revolution (1910-20), continued to be low during the period 1920-40, a fact that helps to explain the relatively sharp increase in percentage of the age group 6 to 14 enrolled in primary school between 1930 (34.3 percent) and 1940 (45.1 percent). With rapid urbanization during and after World War II, these percentages increased to 52.2 percent in 1952 and 55.9 percent in 1960,[13] despite a 3.08 percent population growth rate during the 1950s--a rate that increased still further to 3.45 percent in the early 1960s.[14]

Thus, it is only recently that the basis has been laid for a large and rather rapidly increasing social demand for education at the higher levels. This demand appeared first in the Federal District, and then in more populated states like Nuevo León, but it will have to be dealt with increasingly in the early 1970s in the "provinces" where the universities that are the subject of this study are located. The national percentages of the age group 15 to 19 enrolled in middle education in 1930, 1940, and 1960 were, respectively, 3.4, 6.0, and 12.7, while the comparable percentages in the Federal District were 27, 30, and 37.[15] At the same time, the percentage of the total national enrollment in middle education represented in schools in the Federal District dropped from over 60 percent in 1930 to 39 percent in 1960. High as this latter figure still is, it is clear that more massive social demand for admission to higher education will be felt increasingly in the periphery, particularly since the national institutions in the Federal District have, since 1966, had to restrict admission of persons not residing in the Federal District itself.

The Federal District and the more industrialized areas of the northern states of Mexico continue to benefit from internal migration, the Federal District to the extent of some 650,000 persons during the decade 1950-60.[16] Yet, even with continued migration to the industrial center, the population growth and the gains at the level of primary and secondary education in the periphery will force increased attention to the development of universities outside the capital.

The relatively rapid growth of Mexico's gross national product in the years 1940-70 has been dependent on very rapid industrial growth in a relatively small number of urban areas. The mass of the non-urban population has had a disproportionately small share in the increase in wealth. Investment in human resources in non-urban areas almost inevitably must come from government rather than private sources, but the potential pay-off in terms of increased agricultural productivity and increased consumer demand is high. Yet, in the provinces, investments in education, higher education included, have been small.

FINANCING OF HIGHER EDUCATION IN MEXICO

The financing of higher education in Mexico is highly dependent on the federal government, although the development of the provincial institutions has been, and no doubt will continue to be, dependent in substantial part on state funds. In the late 1960s, about 40 percent of the typical state institution's budget came from state funds, less than 50 percent came from federal funds, and the balance of 15 percent or so came from the institution's own income--normally from rents and very modest tuitions and fees. (Tuition and fees in state institutions usually run no more than $10 to $20 per student per year.) The rough formula for expenditures is that 20 percent of the budget be used for capital investments and the balance for operating expenses, of which roughly 70 percent is earmarked for instruction, 20 percent for research, and 10 percent for adult education and cultural affairs.

Subsidies for public Mexican universities in 1967 are shown in Table 2. The enrollments in university-run programs of study in 1967 are shown in Table 3 (note that most universities manage secondary schools under their budgets).

The number of egresados (those who have completed course work for the professional degree but have not yet completed a thesis) was 8,677 from the institutions in the Federal District and 6,766 from the state universities.[17] The expenditure per enrollee per year in the total system is slightly over 3,000 pesos or about $250. Because of large unassigned administrative expenses in university budgets, it is difficult to get a good cost accounting, as between expenditures for professional students and those in the secondary schools. Nevertheless, by pro-rating general administrative expenses it is possible to estimate roughly that the cost per student per year in the Faculty of Medicine at UNAM or the University of Nuevo León, for example, is on the order of magnitude of $500, while the cost per student per year of instruction at the preparatory level in Yucatán or Oaxaca is well below $100. These figures, like the overall expenditure of $250 per student per year for the entire system, are low in comparative international terms. An OECD estimate of per-pupil recurrent expenditures made in 1964 for the secondary level in Africa and Latin America was

Table 2

Subsidies for Public Mexican Universities, 1967
(in millions of pesos)

	Federal Funds	State Funds	Own Funds	Total
Universities in the Federal District	717	--	40	757
State universities	138	138	113*	389
Total	855	138	153	1,146

*Of this figure, 48 million pesos apply to the Technological Institute of Monterrey alone.

Source: La Educación Superior en México, 1967 (México: ANUIES, 1969), p. 274.

Table 3

Enrollment in University-run Programs of Study, 1967

	Post-graduate	Professional	All Secondary Levels	Total
Universities in the Federal District	2,452	81,035	95,287	178,774
State universities	446	69,781	107,924	178,151
Total	2,898	150,816	203,211	356,925

Source: La Educación Superior en México, 1967 (México: ANUIES, 1969), p. 9.

$250 per year ($200 per year in Asia), while the estimates of per-pupil recurrent expenditures at the level of higher education were $1,000 per year for Africa, $600 per year for Latin America, and $400 per year for Asia.[18]

If one compares subsidies and enrollments in Tables 2 and 3, one notes the coincidence of an approximately equal number of students (178,000+) enrolled in institutions inside and outside the Federal District. Although the latter figure includes a slightly higher proportion of secondary-level students, the striking fact is that the institutions in the Federal District receive almost twice as much total support (757 million pesos as compared to 389 million pesos or about $330 per student per year in the Federal District as compared to about $175 per student per year in the periphery).

The proportion of federal funds going to institutions in the Federal District in 1967 was 84 percent (717 out of 855 million pesos), while the much smaller total going to the states (138 million pesos) was supplemented by an equally small amount from the states themselves. Although some of the state treasuries may be adequate to the task, those in the less developed regions of Mexico clearly are not. Despite the values of autonomy and local support and control, in Mexico the economic facts are that the real possibilities in education, as in other social fields, lie with the budget of the federal government.

In a 1969 article, the Secretary General of ANUIES pointed out that the famous Article 3 and the elaborative Article 73 of the Mexican Constitution provide for the Chief Executive to propose a special law to unify university education throughout the Republic "*en la que se estatuyan las bases generales para unificarla en toda la República*," but such legislation has neither been proposed nor passed.[19] The result at best is a modest financial commitment from the center to the periphery while the possibility of a federally coordinated development of particular types of faculties and programs remains only a theoretical possibility.

Through ANUIES, the universities themselves recently have authorized the creation of the National Planning Center for Higher Education directed by the rectors of UNAM, the National Polytechnical Institute, the seven universities designated as "regional" by ANUIES, and the Secretary General of ANUIES. A secretariat for the commission has been established, but, in the absence of national legislation, the principal power of the group is that of finding facts and making recommendations.

It was in the interest of finding facts that the present study was started, even before the founding of the National Planning Center. The following statement in the Seventh Annual Report of the Social Progress Trust Fund, which was made in reference to all of Latin America, is particularly applicable to the provincial universities of Mexico:

> They [the small institutions of higher education] are an important group if only because of their large number, but they are also important because most of them have been established very recently. It is hoped that at best some of them will grow in importance in the future. From another viewpoint the large number of small new institutions best reflects the ferment that today characterizes higher education in Latin America. Available information is insufficient to establish their real significance but there are grounds for believing that this proliferation of institutions at least in part reflects dissatisfaction and a desire for change, and that even on the basis of number alone they may become stimulant to progress.[20]

The nine universities in the present study are by no means the smallest and least significant of the Mexican universities. On the contrary, the nine universities include five of the principal regional universities and one private institution of international reputation. Although the nine institutions in this study have few resources compared with UNAM, there are some twenty additional provincial universities with even fewer resources than the nine.

Thus, the provincial university of Mexico stands apart historically from the national autonomous universities of Latin America and even from Mexico's own UNAM. The provincial university is equally short of funds but it is younger and, as we shall see, it is not only in the process of rapid growth but also in the process of rapid change and development. As we compare the institutions in our study, it will become evident that the processes of growth and development are by no means synonomous. Perhaps the social demand for admission can be satisfied simply by increasing enrollments and the number of titles bestowed. But the complex new economic and technological demands as well as the demands of rapid social change require qualitative changes (development) within the institution itself. A description of the provincial universities and an analysis of the relationships among the factors of institutional growth, institutional responsiveness, and increasing institutional potential for effective "modern" instruction are the subjects of the following chapters.

NOTES

1. Probably the best single regional analysis for the base year of our study (1967) is the chapter on higher education in Social Progress Trust Fund, Socio-Economic Progress in Latin America, Seventh Annual Report (Washington, D.C.: Inter-American Development Bank, 1968).

2. Ibid., pp. 318, 319.

3. Ibid., p. 384.

4. La Educación Superior en México, 1967 (México: ANUIES, 1969).

5. Social Progress Trust Fund, op. cit., p. 326.

6. La Educación Superior en México, 1966 (México: ANUIES, 1966); Victor L. Urquidi and Adrian Lajous Vargas, Educación Superior, Ciencia y Tecnología en el Desarrollo Económico de México (México: El Colegio de México, 1967).

7. Social Progress Trust Fund, op. cit., p. 319.

8. La Educación Superior en México, 1967, op. cit., pp. 27, 39.

9. Social Progress Trust Fund, op. cit., p. 373.

10. Charles N. Myers, Education and National Development in Mexico (Princeton: Princeton University Press, 1965).

11. Ibid., p. 101.

12. See Ramon Eduardo Ruiz, Mexico, The Challenge of Poverty and Illiteracy (San Marino, Calif.: Huntington Library, 1963).

13. Myers, op. cit., p. 85.

14. Paul Benitez Zenteno and Gustavo Cabrera Acevedo, Projecciones de la Población de México, 1960-1980 (México: Banco de México, 1966), Table 17.

15. Myers, op. cit., p. 93.

16. Gustavo Cabrera, "La Migración Interna en México, 1950-1960," Demografía y Economía, Vol. I (1967), No. 5.

17. Although international comparisons of graduates or graduates as a percentage of enrollments are apt to be fraught with error because of difficulties of definition and collection of comparable data, Mexico seems to have one of the highest rates of graduates in Latin America. However, the percentage of graduates to enrollees, which is slightly over 10 percent (15,443/150,816) still suggests a

good deal of inefficiency. See _UNESCO Yearbook, 1966_ (New York: UNESCO), pp. 180ff., 222ff.

18. _Financing of Education for Economic Growth_ (Paris: OECD, 1966).

19. Alfonso Rangel Guerra, "Las Universidades Mexicanas," _Deslinde_, Vol. IV, August 1969.

20. Social Progress Trust Fund, _op. cit._, p. 323.

CHAPTER

2

THE NINE UNIVERSITIES STUDIED

A DESCRIPTION OF THE UNIVERSITIES

The original design of the study called for a survey of twelve universities, seven designated by ANUIES as regional universities plus an additional five regarded as particularly important to regional development. For a variety of practical reasons that are discussed below, it was possible to obtain questionnaire information from rectors, deans, and professors of only nine of the twelve universities. The nine are: Universidad de Guadalajara, Universidad de Nuevo León, Universidad Autónoma de San Luis Potosí, Universidad de Sonora, Universidad Veracruzana, Universidad de Guanajuato, Universidad Autónoma del Estado de México, Universidad Michoacana de San Nicolás de Hidalgo, and the Instituto Tecnológico y de Estudios Superiores de Monterrey. The first five are designated as regional universities for five of Mexico's seven regions, the last is a privately supported university, and the other three are state-supported institutions located in regions that are also served by the first five.

A detailed analysis of the enrollments of the nine universities under study in comparison with total state and Federal District enrollments is presented in Appendix Table 2. The nine universities enroll somewhat over half of all professional-level students outside the Federal District and produce somewhat over half the total number of graduates. One of them, the Technological Institute of Monterrey, alone enrolls three-quarters of all post-graduate students outside the Federal District. The group of nine thus includes the largest and best established of the provincial universities.

Seven of the nine universities receive financial support, as do most other state universities, in comparable amounts from federal and state sources, although the proportion of state support in the richer states is predictably higher. The Technological Institute of Monterrey is supported almost entirely by tuition, rents, and industrial and private contributions, while the University of Sonora receives a notably large proportion from the state through special taxes. A detailed analysis of sources of income in 1967 is presented in Appendix Table 3.

During the period 1959-66, total expenditures on universities in the states increased from the equivalent of $7 million to $34 million. At the same time, comparable expenditures in the Federal District were increasing from $17 million to $61 million. Increases in expenditures per student over the same period were as follows (pesos per student):[1]

	1959		1966	
In the states	1,151	($92)	1,982	($159)
In the Federal District	2,965	($237)	4,773	($382)

The rate of growth of total support has been great. The rate of growth of support of the individual student has been much more modest, and the level of support of the individual student is still extremely low.

Differences in financing among the nine universities under study are in part related to their system of governance, which, in turn, is partly influenced by their age. The universities of Michoacán (1917), San Luis Potosí (1923), and Guadalajara (1925) were opened during the middle years of the Mexican Revolution (if one thinks of the Mexican Revolution as extending from 1911 through the Cárdenas regime in the late 1930s). The universities of Nuevo León, Sonora, Guanajuato, and Veracruz and the Technological Institute of Monterrey all were established between 1930 and 1950, while the Universidad del Estado de México (1956) is the youngest in the group. As noted earlier, many of the faculties of these universities are much younger than the founding year of the institution may suggest; in fact, over half of all the faculties in these universities were established after 1950. By any criterion, it is a group of very young institutions of higher education.

The state universities of Mexico differ from the older autonomous universities of other Latin American nations in several important respects. As suggested earlier, the movement toward university autonomy that was vitalized (or re-vitalized) in Córdoba, Argentina, in 1918 has a different meaning in Mexico, where a full-scale revolution was already under way and where autonomy, even today some years after the termination of that revolution, less often means an automatic hostility between university and state. The national autonomous universities of other Latin American countries receive a fixed budget from the federal government, often a flat percentage of the budget for total national expenditures. Such budgets ordinarily must be accounted for in fiscal but not in programmatic terms. Decisions about allocations among programs are made entirely within the university, usually by a superior council comprised of a rector, deans, and student and alumni representatives, all of whom are internally elected. By contrast, the provincial universities of Mexico are more closely tied to their respective state governments in the matter of financial and program decisions and even in the appointment of senior university officials.

The University of Sonora, for example, has a *patronato universitario* created in 1953 and composed of private citizens outside the university. This board approves the annual income and expense budgets of the several faculties and is charged with administering and increasing the university's endowment. The Autonomous University of the State of Mexico has a patronato (board of trustees) that was established in 1956 to act as an órgano auxiliar in administering the university's private holdings. It also has the power "to make observations" about budgeted income and expenses before they are acted on by the university council and to designate the internal auditor or controller. A patronato was created for the University of Nuevo León in 1950 as a "decentralized" public corporation to act as the university's financial agent, to handle its private holdings, and, interestingly, to formulate with the university the distribution of the income of those holdings to various activities within the university. The patronato of the Autonomous University of San Luis Potosí, which was created in 1964, also has responsibility for the management of the university's own investments.[2]

With one or two notable exceptions, the patronatos have tended to fulfill the function of supervising the private holdings of the university rather than increasing them. The universities in their turn have sought to increase income by lobbying for more support not only from the regular state and federal sources but also from special local taxes. Thus, the University of Sonora receives its largest share of income from a special 10-percent slice of all taxes received by the state. The Autonomous University of San Luis Potosí receives a special 1.5-percent gasoline tax. The Veracruz University benefits from a special customs tax as well as from special income from its own book stores, its university press, and the state theater, which it operates.

In other words, the provincial universities have to do a good deal of fending for themselves. Receiving the minor share of federal funding, depending in substantial part on very limited regular state funds, and hampered by the lack of a national law to commit the federal government to their development, the universities exist, grow, and change largely in response to a rapidly increasing social demand for access rather than as a result of coordinated inter-university planning. Nevertheless, for their respective states they clearly must play a role comparable in significance to that played by the national universities in their smaller sister nations to the south. If higher-level manpower is a necessity for regional development and if, as seems likely, the local universities must be the source of that manpower, the development of local universities should be a matter of national concern.

The aim of the present study is less to suggest a development plan than to describe certain characteristics of nine of the most important of these peripheral universities. Do they conform to the stereotypes of the smaller national universities in other parts of Latin America that were noted in the Introduction? Is there evidence that they are adapting to growth and change? What seem to be the principal obstacles to their present development? To what extent do they see themselves as related to regional social and economic development and what are they attempting to do about it on their own? What is the evidence of change, growth, and development of instructional capacity within individual university faculties? What characteristics seem to distinguish faculties or universities that are growing and developing from those that are merely growing? How are the factors of qualitative development related to each other and to quantitative growth? It is hoped that the normative and statistical results not only will be of interest to those studying the Latin American university but also can serve the newly formed National Planning Office for Higher Education (Centro Nacional para la Planifación de la Enseñanza Superior) as it begins its important work.

DESIGN OF THE STUDY

The design of the study was drawn up in late 1967 by members of the staff of ANUIES and the Center for Studies in Education and Development of

Harvard University. (Copies of questionnaire materials appear in Appendix B.) Members of the staff of El Colegio de México were consulted on the design of the appendix material drawn from the rectors' questionnaires because the statistical information in that section contains information about the production of high-level manpower in the several regions of the country and is relevant to the regional economic and manpower analyses already undertaken or planned by El Colegio de México.

The original plan for the study called for a questionnaire survey of the rectors and deans and a sample of professors in the seven ANUIES-designated regional universities and in five other universities that also provide major service to several of the regions.

Questionnaire forms for rectors, deans, and professors were pre-tested in one of the major provincial universities in December 1967. On the basis of the pre-test, each of the forms was revised and it was decided to have the deans' and rectors' forms completed through a mail survey and follow-up in the late spring of 1968, with the professors' sample to be obtained through personal visits by members of the ANUIES staff in the fall of 1968. Sixty percent of the completed rectors' and deans' forms were received by July 1968, and the follow-up was in process when it was interrupted by the university strikes of the fall of 1968. Therefore, the visits by the ANUIES staff to member institutions to obtain responses from the sample of professors and the follow-up of rectors' and deans' responses were delayed until the spring of 1969. As a result, completion of coding and analysis in Cambridge, Massachusetts, was delayed to the fall of 1969 because of summer commitments.

The group of nine universities actually analyzed did not include two of the designated regional universities or one other university where it was deemed not feasible to collect questionnaire material. Six of nine rectors completed the full questionnaire, as did 66 of the 87 directors of schools (deans of faculties) in the same nine universities. A summary of returns by faculty type appears in Appendix Tables 4 and 5. The proposed sampling of professors together with the sample actually obtained is reported in Appendix Tables 6 and 7.

The sample of professors was arrived at by an analysis of the statistics for full-time and hourly professors by faculty. The total number of professors in the 87 faculties of the nine universities in 1966 was 3,692, of which 577 or 15 percent were full-time. It was decided to try to obtain an 8-percent sample of the 3,115 hourly (part-time) teachers but also to take a 25-percent "over-sample" of the full-time professors on the ground that they contributed a disproportionately large share of the instruction and because it seemed advisable to include at least one full professor, even from those faculties where the number of full-time professors was very small. ANUIES staff members chose both full-time and hourly professors when they visited the participating universities by applying a table of random numbers to the lists of full-time and part-time professors. Professors then were given the blank questionnaires to fill out and return to the enumerator on the same or the following day.

The major discrepancy between numbers sought and obtained (see Appendix Table 7) is among part-time professors of medicine. Twenty-nine of the "missing" 34 cases are to be found in the very large medical schools of Guadalajara and Nuevo León. Of all part-time professors, those in medicine seem to be the busiest and hardest to reach. Thus, the generalizations about all professors or all professors of medicine in the nine universities under study are affected to the degree that the missing hourly professors in the two medical schools noted above might have affected the various distributions discussed. Full-time professors in faculties of architecture and engineering and in agronomy and veterinary medicine also are slightly under-represented proportionately.

As it happens, 20 of the 183 non-full-time professors are, specifically, half-time rather than hourly professors. Since a number of the conditions of employment of the half-time professor correspond more closely to those of the full-time than to those of the hourly professor, it was decided to transfer those 20 cases from the hourly to the full-time category. Thus, the formal analysis will compare 163 hourly professors with 164 non-hourly professors. The transfer of the 20 half-time professors from a non-full-time to a non-hourly category affects principally the tallies for the universities of San Luis Potosí and Veracruz and those for the schools of medicine, agronomy, and economics.

The somewhat complex manipulation explained above results in a virtually equal number of hourly and non-hourly professors, which facilitates comparisons throughout the analysis without basically distorting the sampling scheme. With the reservations noted, it seems safe to consider the sample of professors as representative of the total population of professors in the nine universities under study. These nine in turn include the larger and, according to the subjective judgment of qualified persons, the better of the provincial universities. As indicated earlier, they enroll 37,000 of the 67,000 students and employ 3,692 of the 6,600 professors in all 24 provincial universities. The sample therefore represents a major part of higher education outside the Federal District.

NOTES

1. La Educación Superior en México, 1966 (México: ANUIES, 1967).

2. Ibid.

CHAPTER 3
RESPONSIVENESS TO REGIONAL NEEDS

AIMS OF THE UNIVERSITY

The descriptions of the Latin American university drawn up by such diverse observers as Rudolph Atcon, a polemical foreign critic, Humberto Cuenca, a militant leftist, Sebastian Mayo, an anti-socialist, and Luis Alberto Sanchez, a moderate enthusiast, to some extent share the view that the Latin American university has not responded to the changing needs of the society but rather has tended to cater to a relatively limited professional elite that is more interested in conservation than change.[1] Obviously, dozens of exceptions must be attached to such a vast generalization. Yet the stereotype persists, particularly in regard to those universities out of the mainstream, outside the capital cities. To what extent does this stereotype apply to the provincial Mexican university? This section will attempt to provide some answers from institutional law and institutional policy as expressed by the rectors of the universities studied.

Each of the Mexican state universities has its own organic law put into effect by its state congress at the time of the founding of the university and in some instances updated to reflect changing practical and legal functions of the university. The laws, as reported in the questionnaires of the six responding rectors (of nine), share the aims of conserving, transmitting, diffusing, enriching, and increasing culture, a traditional set of objectives eloquently argued by José Ortega y Gasset[2] and others. A few of the organic laws make a special point that the benefits of the culture shall be extended to all classes, but in the majority of the cases the aim can be read in the context of the conservative elitist stereotype suggested above.

The second most frequently cited legal aim is the preparation of professionals, an objective still clearly in line with the university's nineteenth-century Napoleonic heritage but amended in the twentieth century with the additional aim of preparing "*investigadores, professores universitarios y técnicos útiles a la sociedad*."

In several provincial universities, the formal aims stop with the transmission of culture and preparation of professionals, but in others a more activist role of the university in society is recognized in such aims as the following:

> Realizar la investigación científica en relación con las necesidades regionales y nacionales. . . . Propiciar la aplicación de los conocimientos científicos en la solución de los problemas estatales y nacionales para mejorar las condiciones de vida del pueblo. . . . Estudiar los problemas actuales de la convivencia humana y particularmente de México. . . . Poner el saber al servicio de la colectividad a traves de un Departamento de Extensión Universitaria. . . . Organizar y llevar a cabo investigaciones principalmente acerca de las condiciones y problemas nacionales y del estado.
>
> [Do scientific research related to regional and national needs. . . . Foster the application of scientific knowledge to the solution of national and state problems in order to improve conditions of the life of

> the people. . . . Study the present problems of human coexistence especially those of Mexico. . . . Place knowledge at the service of the people through a Department of University Extension. . . . Organize and carry out research principally related to the conditions and problems of the state and nation.]

This application of modern science to social problems is a long step from the scientific positivism of late nineteenth-century Mexico, which suggested that existing conditions were to be explained by or, more accurately, explained away by the new science of society. Certainly, the listed aims suggest at least an active intent to deal with social and economic problems.

To the formally stated legal aims of the regional universities, the rectors have added some worthy aims of their own: to develop the indigenous *bellas artes*, to direct instruction more toward public needs, to make tomorrow's leaders in all fields more socially and politically aware, to foster and improve programs for the training of subprofessionals, and to collaborate with other agencies in taking advantage of the available human resources in order to raise the cultural level of the region. Overriding these is the repeated theme of developing pride in the Mexican man and state: "*fortalacer el sentido de mexicanidad*" (strengthen the sense of Mexicanness) and "*que la ciencia y la técnica estén al servicio de los grandes ideales humanisticos de raza, libertad, y justicia*" (let science and technology be at the service of the great humanistic ideals of race, liberty, and justice).

Two themes predominate in the discussion of the university's role in regional development: (1) that it is in the national interest to begin to decentralize the university functions of training and research and (2) that both training and research should reflect the special problems and conditions of the several regions. As one rector puts it:

> La universidad debe contribuir al desarrollo regional no solo aportando los profesionistas y técnicos adecuados al mismo, sino también con trabajos de investigación científica realizadas en función del medio social en que actua, o sea que las Instituciones de Cultura Superior deben ser impulsoras eficientes en la solución de los problemas que en los diversos aspectos de la vida han estado deteniendo el progreso y la elevación de la gran mayoría de nuestra población, especificamente de nuestra población mas escasa en recursos económicos.
>
> [The university ought to contribute to regional development not only by providing the needed professionals and technicians but also through scientific research directed to the social milieu in which it is done. In other words, the institutions of higher culture ought to be efficient forces for the solution of those problems that, in their various forms, have been hampering progress and the improvement of the lot of our population, particularly the poorest members of our population.]

At the philosophical level, the provincial university rectors appear to be committed not only to the traditional functions of the Latin American university--the transmission of culture and the training of professionals--but also to special efforts in regular and extension training and research directed at regional development.

RESPONSIVENESS OF PROGRAMS TO SOCIAL AND ECONOMIC NEEDS

If the university is to play a vital role in regional development, it must not only respond to the demographic growth of the preparatory school population on the one hand and to the quantitative demand for more professionals in the economy on the other; it also must respond qualitatively to changes in the professions themselves, and it must to some degree itself introduce new ideas and new techniques into the professions through its programs of instruction and research.

In an effort to get more specifically and operationally at the responsiveness of the university to the social and economic needs of the region and nation, rectors of the universities and directors of schools (deans of faculties) were asked a number of open-ended questions regarding changes in the practice of the several professions and corresponding changes in professional preparation. Related questions also were asked concerning cooperation with external agencies in planning and teaching regular and extension courses and in carrying out research.

In response to questions about changes in amount and kind of demand for professionals, the rectors were nearly unanimous in pointing out the rising demand for technical personnel, particularly in agronomy and engineering, and the demand for increased sophistication in methodological training. Two rectors went out of their way to point out the growing importance of subprofessional specialties, particularly within the family of engineering specialties but also in the medical and social fields.

One rector felt that the development of a student's social conscience was at least as important as the development of his technical skills:

> Además el papel que deben jugar en las sociedades modernas los abogados y los licenciados en administración de empresas requiere un mayor concepto social de las profesiones en contraposición al antiguo concepto individualista.
>
> [Moreover, the role that lawyers and business administrators ought to play in modern societies requires their thinking of the professions in a social context rather than in the old individualistic way.]

In the rectors' generalizations about program changes made in response to changing demands, it is clear that, although the largest number of changes (usually simple additions) have occurred in the fields of agronomy and engineering, important divisions and rearrangements have been occurring in other fields, especially in science, economics, and medicine. It is equally clear that it has been possible to get special budgetary support for these changes only when such support has been linked directly to increasing enrollments.

Directors of schools responded to similar questions about changes in professional practice and training. The intent of the question about changes in the _profesiones universitarias_ was to elicit opinion about changes in the practice of, rather than the preparation for, the professions, but some misinterpretation did result. Nevertheless, it was possible by examining responses to subsequent questions to record responses for about half the directors, with most respondents listing two or more major types of changes (see Appendix Table 39). It is interesting that the fewest responses came from deans of medicine and law, the best established of the professions. Deans of natural science, engineering, and economics responded with interest and enthusiasm to the question, which is not surprising for these development-related fields. Predictably, the most frequent set of responses had to do with methodological change. Here, the influence of applied mathematics, statistics, operations research, and other systematic methods was frequently mentioned; one director stated: "We are now in an era of predictive science rather than _post hoc_ empiricism."

The third most frequently mentioned changes were those of general technical advance and changes in the technical materials available to the various professions. Also stressed was the need for the given profession to develop the skills and facilities for research that would permit the profession to _produce_ change.

The directors who pointed to changes in demand were sensitive both to the need for increased numbers of professionals as a result of demographic growth and to the need for new kinds of specialists. A few also indicated that sheer social demand for entry into the university and the limited capacities of the traditional faculties had been forces for the creation of new carreras, which, in turn, had occasioned changes in the practice of the professions. This comes about as much from the creation of new subprofessional carreras as from the creation of professional-level carreras, since the availability of subprofessionals tends to upgrade the practice of the parent profession.

Cited least often, except by the deans of economics, but to us the most original suggestions about the nature of change in the professions, were those concerning new social needs and the fundamentally new ways in which the society was catering to those needs through its government. It was suggested that urbanization not only increases social needs but also changes their character. For example, migrants to cities from rural areas suddenly need to acquire a whole new set of skills for survival in the city. The government is intervening in more areas of life and will necessarily be increasingly involved in social and economic development in the future. The "importancia de administración, planeación y programación" is growing--all of which has rather fundamental implications for the practice of and training for the professions.

The directors were asked to comment on the causes of the changes they saw in the practice of their professions. The 33 of 67 directors who responded emphasized the effect that newly taught professional and research skills have on society. The possession of new skills almost inevitably means a change in the professional's approach to his practice. Conversely, the directors also noted that the new order of skills demanded by today's complex economic and social systems was forcing changes in the substance and methods of professional training.[3]

Although only half the directors commented on changes in the practice of their respective professions, over two-thirds of the professors sampled had opinions on the subject. In general, the professors' responses paralleled those of the directors (see Appendix Table 39), with the largest response coming from professors of natural sciences, engineering, and economics. Professors, more than directors, emphasized specific technical advances, particularly advances in methodology or software. Neither professors nor directors often referred to the function of research except in the faculties of medicine, engineering, and agronomy. Curiously, responses dealing with the effect of the increasing activities of government on the professions came from professors of medicine rather than from professors of economics or law, who are supposedly the most expert in these matters.

Eighty percent of the professors indicated that they had changed their courses in response to changes in the profession. Most replies were concerned with the reorganization of topics and, in an unspecified way, with raising the level and quality of instruction. A minority of professors of medicine, science, engineering, and economics emphasized the introduction of specific new techniques, new conceptual approaches, and new mathematical methodologies, but most responses were disappointingly general. Although there were a few specific instances of increased emphasis on the empirical and the practical in instruction, in response to an open-ended question virtually no mention was made of the importance of training and experience in research in an undergraduate professional program.

Non-hourly professors responded in somewhat greater numbers than hourly professors to the inquiry about course changes, but the changes cited by the two groups were almost identical.

Just as professors were asked about course changes, so deans were asked about program changes. The deans, like the professors, reported changes that seem more organizational than substantive in nature.

Modifications seem to have been simple additions or rearrangements of courses rather than efforts to redirect the students' approach to learning.

It is important to note that the deans surveyed oversee faculties or schools of which the great majority were founded after 1950 (see Appendix Table 37), and that they administer programs of study of which the majority were officially revised after 1965. Presumably, the younger the faculty, the less historical baggage it must carry. Programs in law and medicine, like schools of law and medicine, are older than the rest, but even the majority of these revised their programs of study in the 1960s. Law and medicine tend to have only one professional program within a given faculty, but engineering and the natural sciences not only have spawned numerous types of faculties but also have an average of two or three separate degree programs within a given faculty. Notable by their relative absence are the shorter non-degree courses of three years' duration or less.[4] In general, the short courses are of recent origin and the effective date of particular programs is apt to mark the beginning of a new program rather than the revision of an older one.

The revision of professional programs is not an on-going process in most Latin American universities, a fact that can be clearly inferred from a comparison of current catalog descriptions of programs with those reported in the systematic analysis of programs throughout Latin America undertaken by the Unión de Universidades Latinoamericanas in 1952.[5] In the majority of universities, the principal changes are merely additions. New faculties are created or new _carreras_ (programs) are created within faculties, but the new programs are fairly fixed and rigid and have few course options and little or no possibility of transfer of credit from one faculty to another or even from one program to another.

It was of interest to discover, therefore, whether the universities in our study had merely rearranged relatively fixed programs, or whether they, like UNAM, had been experimenting with transfer of credit or other forms of intra- and even inter-institutional cooperation. In general, the response was negative.[6]

The only substantial movement toward cooperative programs in the provincial universities seems to be in the faculties of medicine and natural sciences, with surprisingly little participation from engineering despite its common scientific interests. Where cooperative arrangements do exist, they tend to exist with more than one other faculty, but again this is primarily in the faculties of medical and natural sciences. The cooperation that does go on between and among faculties seems to be evenly divided between exchange of professors and exchange of credit.[7]

Concerning future forms of cooperative arrangements for instruction, directors saw some likelihood of the formation of departments and a greater use of inter-institutional as opposed to inter-faculty exchanges (see Appendix Table 38). Suggestions for departmentalization came primarily from deans of natural science and engineering. Only two deans of law and two deans of philosophy responded to the item.

In commenting on present forms of inter-faculty cooperation, most of the rectors indicated that some interchange of professors among faculties, and particularly interchange of professors among programs within faculties, was operative. Apparently, efforts are also being made toward the joint purchase and use of transportation (including buses for students) and laboratory and machine-shop equipment and the joint use of classroom and laboratory buildings. But, with one or two exceptions, regular use of transfer credit from faculty to faculty is just beginning to be tried. As one rector said:

> Las asignaturas deben cursarse y cubrirse en la escuela en que el alumno está matriculado, solo rara y excepcionalmente se permite cursar alguna materia bajo programa similar en otra escuela.

[Courses must be taken in the student's own faculty. Only rarely is he permitted to take a course given by a similar program in another faculty.]

Most rectors, however, did look to increased interchange of professors and of credits in the future.

Most of the directors felt that the program changes in the late 1960s were indeed in response to external changes in the profession. All the universities do seem to have been involved in at least some program change (a fact also to be inferred from Appendix Table 37).[8] Among faculty types, the natural and economic sciences seem to be pressing most actively for change; law and medicine appear to be least inclined to press for change.

Professors and directors thus indicated that most program and course changes are organizational rather than pedagogical in nature. New or more sophisticated methodology and practical applications of theory and research findings seem to be of secondary importance.[9] The reorganization of programs is often the addition of a new carrera, the addition of new courses, the addition of an academic year, the shifting of material from one year to another, the fusion of two carreras into one, or the combination of courses--in short, administrative changes rather than the reworking of the substance of a present carrera. Changes seem more apt to occur in the newer faculties and in programs that have not yet "solidified." Almost no mention was made of attempts to change the learning habits of students except by implication in the inclusion of more methodological and practical material in the curriculum. But methodology is usually talked of as yet another materia to be mastered, rather than as a tool for self-learning (autodidaxis).

THE INSTITUTION AND THE COMMUNITY

The most important changes in the substance and methodology of regular instructional programs undoubtedly have come about through the advanced training of professors. Yet useful change also can result from the advice and participation of individuals and organizations outside the university. Most of the university rectors reported some arrangement with outside organizations and agencies in planning and administering regular instructional programs, although one said flatly "no hay" (there aren't any). The most typical arrangement is supervised preprofessional practice for nurses, social workers, or doctors in local hospitals and social service agencies. One rector traced the history of negotiations between the university and the Association of Cattle and Hog Raisers (Unión de Ganaderos y Porcicultores), which resulted in the recent founding of a new faculty of veterinary medicine and zootechnics. In this instance, the demand for new types of trained professionals and applied research was effectively expressed to the university in direct fashion. Other universities report the assistance of private foundations in helping establish new programs, particularly in the natural sciences.

The deans of faculties (directors of schools) echoed the reports of the rectors regarding outside cooperation in planning and instruction in regular programs, but only half indicated the regular participation of outside groups.[10] Faculties of engineering and agronomy are most active; faculties of law and philosophy have the least outside cooperation. Almost all faculties at the Technological Institute of Monterrey and the University of Guanajuato receive outside advice and cooperation in program planning.

Most common "outside" arrangements reported by directors[11] to improve the regular programs include the previously mentioned internship arrangements with hospitals and other social agencies plus technical consultations on research and teaching with other Mexican institutions, particularly UNAM and El Colegio de México (Mexico's independent graduate school of social sciences and humanities). Similar arrangements are made with professional associations; exchange of credits is sometimes effected with other faculties and universities; and relations with private and international agencies are not unusual.

In general, arrangements for outside assistance in the planning and operation of regular courses of instruction are relatively recent in origin: Over half were started in 1964 or later. Most common reported source of special funding for advice and assistance with programs of instruction is the federal government, and the department's own funds are the second most common source. Foreign foundations and corporations provided the third largest specified source; private Mexican funds and UNAM funds also are used. The balance of reported cases involve single instances of funding from state and municipal funds, a combination of university and outside funding, funding from elsewhere within the university, and foreign government support. Faculties of engineering and natural sciences are the most active in providing course instruction for interested outside groups.

In addition to soliciting advice and consultation (asesoría) from outside sources regarding programs of instruction, one-third of the faculties under study cooperate with outside groups in providing courses for the community.[12] These are largely adult education courses, in-service training for teachers, and special courses for state and federal agencies, particularly in the fields of public health and social welfare. The programs seem to be relatively recent in origin: The majority were started after 1964, and only four of the reported programs were organized prior to 1960. In general, the directors indicated that the individual faculties absorb the costs of the programs in their own budgets, although funding also is obtained from external public and private agencies and foundations, from tuition and fees, and from central university sources.

In discussing programs of community service, the rectors emphasize courses for the padres de familia, usually in cooperation with the Institute of Social Security. These courses, together with adult courses in literacy and cultural programs for young adults, apparently are offered not only through the individual faculties but also through the university's preparatory school, using the school's facilities (and sometimes its teachers) during the evening hours. The university's response to the community thus is not limited solely to its professional-level faculties and research institutes. If the response is by no means universal, it is active, diverse, and growing. Numerous innovative ideas are implicit in the arrangements described. The Latin American university stereotype of aloof and isolated professional faculties clearly is much less applicable today than it was even five years ago.

RESEARCH AND REGIONAL DEVELOPMENT

Just as change in instruction has been facilitated by certain internal and external administrative arrangements, research has received a stimulus from new organizational arrangements.

In response to a question about university-wide efforts to foster or coordinate research, the rectors in general pointed to the several research institutes in a given university. Typically, these institutes are in the areas of medicine, engineering, natural sciences, and economics and they are attached to particular faculties. In several universities, however, there is a more comprehensive "Institute (or Center) of Scientific Investigation" or a "Council for Scientific Research" charged to "_fomentar, coordinar, promover y difundir la investigación científica y sus resultados_." A few special-purpose research institutes or programs--such as the Instituto de Investigación de Zonas Desérticas at the University of San Luis Potosí or the research in marine resources among numerous generalized research efforts at the Centro de Investigaciones Científicas y Tecnológicas at the University of Sonora--attempt to cross disciplinary and professional lines in an attack on broad substantive areas.[13]

Research described by directors of schools[14] seemed somewhat less inspiring than that described by rectors, but two-thirds of the directors (44) did indicate that research was regularly carried out in their faculties. Universities reported about equal proportions of faculties engaged in research, except one that reported no research activities and one (Technological Institute of Monterrey) in which every faculty had on-going research projects. About 200 specific faculty research projects were listed by the 44 deans who responded affirmatively. The projects were equally divided between research related to instruction and research not so related.[15] Of course, deans probably did not have lists of faculty research publications at hand when filling out the questionnaire. But even as a somewhat biased sample, the reported figures are low. This is not surprising in light of heavy teaching, advising, and administrative loads and in view of the economic pressures of low salaries and the necessity of outside work to supplement income. Our interest here is to discover whether there are other constraints to research.

In much of Latin America, what research is carried on takes place within research institutes that may or may not be part of a teaching faculty and that employ researchers who may or may not also be teaching professors. Even the fact that a researcher is a teaching member of a faculty does not insure that students will participate in his research. The Latin American view of research often corresponds to that expressed by the Spanish philosopher-journalist, José Ortega y Gasset, that research is a technical activity to be engaged in by a few whose cultural and professional "formation" is already complete. The corollary is that research is not an area of concern for the general student, even in the later years of his professional training.[16] This is in sharp contrast to the view of the university expressed by the German scientist-philosopher, Karl Jaspers, for whom the primary mission of the university is neither transmitting the culture nor providing clinical training but providing methodological tools and the occasion to engage in original investigation with a master teacher-researcher.[17]

To what extent do the Mexican deans of faculties see research as a necessary or desirable part of instruction and learning? Of the 66 deans, 29 explained how research is related to instruction in their schools. The majority (18) indicated that it forms part of the instruction in certain advanced seminars where students are required to do original work or have the opportunity to build new equipment or work together on a practical project. Only 4 indicated that original research was a required element of the thesis for the degree. Others noted that formal research was part of clinical training. Some suggested that a faculty rule that professors produce some new research each year led to the use of student assistants. Two deans reported that research was related to instruction through the professor's lecture notes, which he regularly uses to describe his own research results and those of others. If the description of student involvement in research does not suggest a graduate school of arts and sciences, neither does it suggest the isolated research institute described in much of the literature on the Latin American university (see Further Reading).

A third of the deans indicated that research was done in cooperation with other institutions. In only the medical and natural science faculties did more than half the deans report such arrangements. As with special arrangements for instruction, the most common external sponsorship or cooperation for research appears to come from the federal agencies or commissions like the National Institutes of Petroleum, Nuclear Energy, or Scientific Technological and Agricultural Research (11 examples cited).

The second most frequent type of external collaboration in research is with foreign universities, with such foundations as Ford and Rockefeller, and with such inter- or Pan-American organizations as the Comité Latinoamericano de Escuelas de Administración (6 specific arrangements listed). Research arrangements with other Mexican institutions appear to be less numerous, but 3 instances of collaborative work with UNAM and El Colegio de México were cited. State agencies, hospitals, and cultural institutes provided additional occasions for research (5 examples listed), while industries, cooperatives (e.g., mining cooperatives), and private agencies, particularly private agencies for tourism, are the source of an equal number of external cooperative arrangements for research. Finally, 6 examples are given of cooperative research undertaken with other faculties or with quasi-independent research institutes within the same university.

The principal source of research funding is the individual contracting agency, particularly the federal agencies and the several research institutes at UNAM (16 cases), with donations from international foundations, inter-American agencies and foreign universities (7 responses) next. Much of the research done in collaboration with outside entities is financed by the university itself (3 cases), by the school undertaking the research (4 cases), by the professors themselves (5 cases), or by students (3 cases). Some universities require each professor to produce one piece of research per year, and the student is often asked to finance all or part of his thesis research.

It is very difficult to ascertain actual expenditures for research because so many expenditures are absorbed by professors and students and because the accounting procedures within universities do not always make a separate cost accounting of this item, particularly that portion supported by external funds. Victor L. Urquidi and Adrian Lajous Vargas report that about $12.5 million (156 million pesos) was available for scientific research and development in Mexico in 1964. Of this total, about $3.2 million was spent on agricultural research, $2.1 million on industrial research, $1.4 million on the National Commission of Nuclear Energy, $.8 million on medical research, $1.8 million for research done under the auspices of the National Polytechnical Institute, and $2.2 million for research done under the auspices of UNAM, with the balance in miscellaneous activities.[18] The importance to the provincial universities of funds for agricultural, nuclear, and medical research, as well as the more general research funds of UNAM is reflected in the replies to the questionnaire. The funds from the National Polytechnical Institute and the funds for industrial research are mentioned less frequently. In any case, the share of the provincial universities in this research activity is relatively small and, as Urquidi and Lajous point out, the total in national terms is very small in the first place.

The majority of arrangements for sponsored research in the provincial universities were established after 1964, although almost 30 percent antedate 1960. Certainly, allocations to research at the national level since 1964 have had some impact on the provincial universities, particularly on the medical and natural science faculties.

When asked what incentives were offered to professors to conduct research, 55 of the 66 directors answered frankly, "None." The 11 directors who did respond affirmatively cited academic promotion (mentioned 5 times) and a reduced teaching load (mentioned 4 times) as the most important rewards for research productivity, with increase in salary and fellowships for graduate study given as the other principal incentives. *Ad hoc* pay for research, the possibility of royalties, and trips to meetings also were mentioned as incentives. Policies in support of these incentives were reported to be relatively recent in origin, dating back only three or four years on the average. Of the 11 deans reporting incentives to research, 3 were in medical faculties and 2 each were in engineering and economics faculties. All 5 of the deans reporting from Monterrey mentioned one or more incentives to research for professors as a matter of regular policy.

Despite the relative lack of formal incentives to research and scholarship, returns from our sample of professors corroborate the deans' reports of increased research activity. A surprising 25 percent of the sample reported publishing at least one "book" since 1963, with productivity distributed among fields as indicated in Appendix Table 19.

Of course, there is some room for interpretation as to what is and what is not a book, and it is clear that some professors considered bound volumes of their lecture notes (*apuntes*) as books. Nevertheless, the production is still substantial and belies the picture of the taxi professor who spends the minimum time possible on his course and his academic self-development.[19]

Of the 327 professors in the sample, 80 had published one or more journal articles since 1963, a figure somewhat less striking than the number claiming to have published books. Medical faculties again enjoyed the lead[20] (see Appendix Table 20). Over one-third of the professors listed unpublished research, with the largest relative contributions coming from medicine and economics and from non-hourly professors.[21]

However meager the incentives, some professors are producing research and university administrations are trying to help them, organizationally if not financially. Here too, the movement is recent but impressive.

A majority of provincial university rectors and professors and a substantial minority of deans seem to be sensitive to change outside the university, sensitive not only to changes in the practice of their respective professions but also to social, economic, and technological change. Most sensitive, interested, and active in responding programmatically to these changes are the professors and deans of economics, natural sciences, and engineering. Most responsive to the idea of regional service through research are deans and professors of medicine, economics, and agronomy. Notable differences also exist among universities, with the Technological Institute of Monterrey most active in interaction with the community in both instructional programs and research. Professional research publication also is relatively high at the universities of Sonora, Guadalajara, Nuevo León, San Luis Potosí, and Veracruz. But institutional incentives to professors to do research are notably lacking and outside support is spotty.

Programs apparently are revised with a fairly high degree of regularity, particularly in faculties of natural science and economics. But revision seems to be more organizational than substantive or methodological in nature, and it relatively seldom involves instructional cooperation with other faculties except in the cases of medicine and natural sciences.

Thus, the provincial university is considerably more responsive to the changing needs of the society than the stereotypes would have it. However, great variation exists both among universities and among types of faculties in the amount and kind of response, and lack of financial resources to support university participation in regional development is clearly a problem.

NOTES

1. Rudolph Atcon, The Latin American University (Bogotá: Editorial ABC, 1966); Humberto Cuenca, La Universidad Revolucionaria (Caracas: Editorial Contemporanea, 1964); Sebastian Mayo, La Educación Socialista en México: El Asalto a la Universidad Nacional (Rosario, Argentina: Editorial Bear, 1964); Luis Alberto Sanchez, La Universidad Latinoamericana (Guatemala: Editorial Universitaria, 1954).

2. José Ortega y Gasset, Mission of the University (Princeton: Princeton University Press, 1944).

3. The 33 responses to the question about causes of change in the practice of the profession included the following: political stability permits change (1); the modern complexities of economic and administrative life demand new skills and procedures (6); changes can be explained primarily by new kinds of social needs (5); the existence of a research capacity makes change inevitable (4); and the greater variety of skills possessed by practitioners is a guarantee that change will take place (17).

4. For a more complete analysis of the facts and consequences of the lack of subprofessional technical programs within Mexican higher education, see Russell G. Davis, Scientific, Engineering and Tech-

nical Education in Mexico (New York: Education and World Affairs, 1967).

5. Planes de Estudios de las Universidades Latinoamericanas (Guatemala: Unión de Universidades Latinoamericanas, 1952).

6. Thirty-five of the 66 directors responded to the question, but 15 of the responses indicated either that there was no cooperation among faculties or that, if there was cooperation, it was strictly informal and unofficial. Five of the medical deans reported cooperation with other faculties, 2 with natural science faculties and the rest with the medical or dental specialties. Seven natural science deans reported cooperative programs, 2 with other natural science faculties, 4 with one or more engineering faculties, and one with a specialized school in the "philosophy" category. Only 4 of the engineering faculties reciprocated, 2 with schools of natural science, one with another engineering faculty, and one with a specialized philosophy faculty. Only one dean of agronomy, 2 deans of economics, and one dean of philosophy reported formal cooperative relationships, and all deans of law responded negatively. (For F test among faculty types, $p = .002$; among universities, $p = .17$--not significant.)

The F test results from a one-way analysis of variance in which the variance among groups is compared in a ratio to the variance within groups. The p value is a statement of how often a ratio as large as the one observed could have occurred by chance alone. As the p value approaches .00, we can be more and more confident that a real difference exists among the groups being compared.

7. Of the 29 instances of cooperation among 20 faculties (of the 66 faculties in the nine provincial universities studied), 16 involved the exchange of credit, 9 the exchange of professors, and 4 the exchange of both. Six deans pointed out that their departmental structure had built into it a system for the exchange of credit, and an additional 6 noted that, although there was no program cooperation,

there was cooperation in the use of physical facilities. (For F test among faculty types on number of instances of cooperation, p = .09--not significant; among universities, p = .75--not significant.)

In answer to the question of what the directors thought about various types of cooperation (as opposed to reporting the fact of cooperative arrangements), the response was more positive: 46 of the directors responded and only 6 of them indicated potential difficulties in accomplishing cooperation--usually because of allegedly different approaches or different levels of instruction among separate faculties. The great majority (26) gave responses that suggested a feeling that the experience of interchanging professors was desirable in that it improved relationships and led to the self-improvement of professors, as well as providing students with some elective courses: Six directors pointed out the economic benefits that accrue from cooperative use of professors and physical facilities, and 4 indicated the academic benefits that would accompany departmentalization.

8. The proportions of directors indicating changed programs were as follows: medicine, 6/11; natural sciences, 10/10; architecture and engineering, 12/16; agronomy and veterinary medicine, 2/4; economics and business administration, 10/11; law, 3/7; and philosophy and others, 4/7. Comparable figures by university are Guanajuato, 5/6; Guadalajara, 8/11; Estado de México, 6/8; Michoacán, 2/4; Nuevo León, 5/8; the Technological Institute of Monterrey, 5/5; San Luis Potosí, 6/8; Sonora, 3/6; and Veracruz, 7/10. (For F test among faculty types, p = .07--possibly significant; among universities, p = .78--not significant.)

9. Of the more than 70 specific changes cited by 38 directors, the most common was a change in the organization of the carrera (35). Other changes were: the introduction of a more sophisticated methodology (13); more emphasis on the practical and pragmatic (9); inclusion of new non-technical material (8); introduction or revision of a credit system (2); instruction linked to research (1); and

greater attention to the individual, presumably through a program of orientación or guidance (1).

10. About half (32) of the directors indicated that their schools had some connection with organizations or agencies outside the university in the planning or operation of instructional programs. Faculties of engineering (10/16) and agronomy (3/4) were most active in this respect, while law (2/7) and philosophy (2/7) were least involved. Universities indicating the largest proportion of reporting faculties participating with agencies outside the university in the planning or operation of programs were Guanajuato (5/6) and the Technological Institute of Monterrey (4/5). (F tests were not computed.)

11. There was a total of 53 responses on the nature of the outside cooperation in the planning and instruction of regular courses: relations with international institutions (universities), industries, and foundations (5); with other Mexican institutions, particularly UNAM and El Colegio de México, for technical consultation (asesoría técnica) on teaching programs and research as well as for cursillos or short courses (8); with professional associations (6); with sister faculties in other universities for the exchange of credits or professors (8); with private enterprises and associations like the Asociaciones de Hoteles or the Agencies de Viajes (10); and with national, state, and municipal governmental agencies all the way from organizations like the Institución de Protección a la Infancia del Estado or the Hospital de Marina to the Departamento Nacional de Turismo or the Banco de México (16).

12. Eighteen of the 67 directors indicated that their schools offered courses for federal agencies, particularly in the following areas: public health and social welfare (6); miscellaneous, short, noncredit courses for adults in the community (9); inservice courses for teachers and professors (5); and courses for the local chamber of commerce or local industries (2). (Four of the 18 directors reported 2 programs.)

Principal sources of financing for the community courses were the school (faculty) providing the service course (7); private industry (3); private foundations (2); tuition or fees from the participants (2); the state (1); and the university from its central funds (1). One program was operated without charge with professors contributing their services.

13. The response from the University of Sonora is particularly interesting:

> La Universidad cuenta con el Centro de Investigaciones Científicas y Tecnológicas. Actualmente está cubriendo en su primera etapa de desarrollo actividades de investigación en los campos de la Química Inorgánica, Química Orgánica, Biología, Energía Solar, Desalación de Agua del Mar, Hidroponia, Metalurgía e Ingeniería de Procesos. Sus proyectos actuales de investigación son:
>
> 1. Construcción y operación de la Planta Pilóto para concentrar minerales radioactivos del Noroeste de México. Objetivo: Investigar la composición, características y tecnologías aplicadas a los minerales radioactivos del Noroeste de México para obtener información básica de diseño para la construcción de plantas industriales.
>
> 2. Proyectos de investigación para el desarrollo de los recursos marinos del Golfo de California. Objetivos: Investigar las características y aprovechamiento integral del camarón y totoaba; conocer las condiciones oceanográficas de la zona Norte del Golfo y establecer una Estación de Tecnología de Alimentos Marinos.
>
> 3. Obtención de cobre metálico. Concentrados de cobre de alta ley mediante el proceso de fluidización y termociclón. Objetivos: Aprovechar los abundantes minerales oxidados de cobre de Sonora.

4. Investigación de invernaderos de ambiente controlado. Objetivo: Desarrollar comunidades desérticas costeras autosuficientes en agua, energía y alimentos.

5. Estudio fitoquímico de las plantas del desierto de Sonora.

6. Investigación del aprovechamiento de la gobernadora.

7. Investigación de materias primas agrícolas susceptibles de fermentación industrial.

8. Evolución de la flora marina en la Zona Noroeste del Golfo de California.

9. Fermentación del maguey de Sonora para obtención de bacanora.

10. Investigación del aprovechamiento de la cañagría.

11. Investigación de nuevos proyectos a base de trigo. Es el Centro de practica y adiestramiento de los alumno que estudian en la Escuela de Ciencias Químicas.

[The university has a Center for Scientific and Technological Research. At the moment, it is in the first stages of developing research activities in the fields of inorganic chemistry, organic chemistry, biology, solar energy, desalination of seawater, hydroponics, metallurgy, and process engineering. Its present research projects are:

1. Construction and operation of a pilot plant to bring together radioactive materials from Northwest Mexico. Object: to investigate the composition, characteristics, and possible technological applications of the radioactive minerals of Northwest Mexico with an eye to the design and future construction of industrial plants.

2. Research projects aimed at the development of the marine resources of the Gulf of California. Objectives: to investigate the characteristics and potential utilization of shrimp and other shellfish; to learn more about the oceanographic conditions of the northern zone of the Gulf; and to establish a Station for the Technology of Marine Foods.

3. The extraction of metallic copper. Concentration of copper of high quality through a process of fluidization and thermal agitation. Objectives: to capitalize on the abundant sources of oxidized copper in Sonora.

4. Research on hothouses with controlled environment. Objective: to develop communities in the coastal desert region that are self-sufficient in water, energy, and food.

5. Phytochemical study of the plants of the desert of Sonora.

6. Research on the utilization of certain types of fish.

7. Research on prime agricultural materials susceptible to industrial fermentation.

8. Research on the evolution of marine flora in the northwest zone of the Gulf of California.

9. Research on the fermentation of the maguey [century] plant of Sonora for the purpose of obtaining certain extracts.

10. Research on the utilization of sugar-cane products.

11. Research on new wheat-based products. This is being done through a center for the practical training of the students in the School of Chemical Sciences.]

14. Directors were asked about research in their schools and arrangements for financing same. Two-thirds (44) indicated that research was systematically conducted with the following proportion of directors responding affirmatively: medicine, 9/11; natural sciences, 7/10; engineering, 8/16; agronomy, 3/4; economics and business administration, 6/11; law, 5/7; and philosophy, 6/7.

15. Of the dozen faculties reporting more than five formal pieces of research completed in the previous three years, three were faculties of medicine, two were faculties of natural sciences, and four were faculties of philosophy and letters.

16. Ortega y Gasset, _op. cit_.

17. Karl Jaspers, _The Idea of the University_ (Boston: Beacon Press, 1959).

18. Victor L. Urquidi and Adrian Lajous Vargas, _Educación Superior, Ciencia y Tecnología en el Desarrollo Económico de México_ (México: El Colegio de México, 1967), p. 58.

19. Of the 163 hourly professors, 32 reported publishing at least one book as compared with 53 of 164 non-hourly professors. Of the 85 professors listing published books, 27 are at the Technological Institute of Monterrey, 11 at Guadalajara, and 10 each at Nuevo León and San Luis Potosí. (For F tests among faculty types, $p = .07$; among universities, $p = .04$.)

20. Of the 80 professors publishing articles, 28 were hourly and 52 non-hourly, which conforms to common sense prediction. The largest percentage of professors writing articles was to be found at Sonora (38 percent) and the Technological Institute of Monterrey (34 percent). Of the 25 professors

writing more than 5 articles, 10 were employed at the Technological Institute of Monterrey and 5 at Nuevo León. (For F test among faculty types, p = .10; among universities, p = .006.)

21. In our sample, 120 of 327 professors had produced various types of unpublished research since 1963, with the largest numbers in the fields of medicine (23) and economics (25) and the smallest number (10) in law. Roughly two-thirds of non-hourly professors and one-third of hourly professors had produced at least one piece of as yet unpublished research. Sonora and the Technological Institute of Monterrey led the list of universities on this item with 50 percent of their professors responding affirmatively; San Luis Potosí (45 percent) and Veracruz (40 percent) followed next. (For F test among faculty types, p = .04; among universities, p = .56--not significant.)

CHAPTER

4

INSTRUCTIONAL CAPACITY

A truly valid description and analysis of the process of teaching and learning in the provincial universities would, of course, require the direct observation of the habits of professors and students as they go about their work in and out of class. For a variety of reasons, this sort of study was simply not practicable and we have been forced to rely on indirect evidence from questionnaire responses and objective statistical information drawn from other university sources. In short, we have had to look at the institutions' potential or capacity for effective instruction rather than at instruction itself.

THE PROFESSOR

As indicated in Chapter 3, a substantial fraction of the provincial university faculties are attempting, through research and instruction, to respond to and to lead their regions in a variety of forms of social and economic development. What are the professorial talents with which they have to work? How are such talents found, fostered, and rewarded? What is the educational background of the professor in the provincial Mexican university; how was he recruited into teaching; how is he continuing to develop himself; what incentives are provided to him; what handicaps must he overcome? In other words, what is the university's instructional capacity?

Background

The first notable characteristic of the provincial professor is that he is overwhelmingly likely to be male. Only 10 professors in our sample of 327 were women. This is perhaps not too surprising since, in most nations, university teaching (as opposed to primary and secondary teaching) usually is a distinctly male profession. Furthermore, in Mexico the proportion of women to men enrolled as students in higher education is small even by Latin American standards. According to the most recent ANUIES report, of 150,000 students enrolled at the professional level of higher education only 25,000, or 16 percent, were women. The combined enrollments of fifth- and sixth-year university students totaled 16,000; only 2,000, or 12.5 percent, were women.[1] Interestingly enough, the largest number of women were not enrolled in faculties of humanities, philosophy, and pedagogy but in medical, biological, dental, and pharmaceutical sciences, accounting, and law; these data suggest that in Mexico secondary school teaching, like university teaching, is very much a male profession. Certainly, this must be true of the _preparatoria_ run by the universities. (The training of primary school teachers takes place in normal schools outside the universities and is not considered in this study.)

Mexico's percentage of university enrollment of women (16 percent) is nearly identical to that in Honduras (15 percent), Guatemala (16 percent), and Bolivia (16 percent) but is in sharp contrast to university enrollment of women in Panama (46 percent), Uruguay (42 percent), Argentina (39 percent), and Chile (38 percent).[2] One might suspect that the proportion of women in higher education in the modern industrialized Federal District would be higher than in the states, but this does not seem to be the case. In the Federal District, 13,786 (17 percent) of 81,035 students are women, while in the states the figure is

11,408 (16 percent) of 69,781 students.[3] Women apparently play a relatively small role in preparatory-level teaching even in the Federal District. Even in the medical sciences where enrollment of women is relatively heavy (5,000 of 25,000 university women are in medicine and dentistry), their numbers are small in comparison to the 18,000 men in training for the same profession. This is a substantially larger proportion of women in medical sciences than in the United States, but it is only about one-fourth of the percentage in the Soviet Union where 80 percent of doctors are women. Clearly, Mexico has not yet begun to utilize women in higher-level occupations at anything like potential rates, and the almost infinitesimal number of women professors in our sample emphasizes this fact.

The second notable fact about professors in Mexican provincial universities is their youth. Half of the professors in our sample graduated from the preparatoria in 1953 or later, and the same number received their first professional degrees in 1959 or later. These data suggest that almost half of all professors were under 30 years of age in 1967 (see Appendix Table 8). Half of the 131 professors who had obtained a graduate degree had received it in 1964 or later.

Median graduation dates from preparatory school and first university program vary somewhat by faculty type, as indicated in Appendix Table 9. Although all types of faculties have surprisingly young professors, the more traditional faculties of law and medicine have teaching faculties a good decade older than the average. No doubt these data are related to the dates at which the individual faculties were established.[4]

Once again, the stereotype must be adjusted to fact. Mexican professors are not the anticipated over-aged practitioners hanging onto their cátedras (chairs) for life but rather youthful recent graduates bent on continuing their education and self-development.

Training

Professors tended to have attended public (69 percent) rather than private (31 percent) junior high schools and public (78 percent) rather than private (22 percent) high schools, or _preparatoria_. (In Mexico, about half the high schools are attached to the public universities, a fact that may explain the reduced number going to private schools at that level.)

About 10 percent of the provincial university professors attended _secundaria_ in the Federal District and about 4 percent attended school at this level outside Mexico. As might be expected, the great majority (over 75 percent) of professors attended _secundaria_ in the regions in which their universities are located, as indicated in Appendix Table 10. The pattern persists at the _preparatoria_ level (see Appendix Table 11), although a substantial number of those now teaching at the universities of the Estado de México, Michoacán, and Veracruz moved to the Federal District for their pre-university training, raising the total percentage of professors who attended _preparatoria_ in the Federal District to 15. A substantial shift to the Federal District also occurred at the undergraduate (professional) level of the university (see Appendix Table 12), with 23 percent of all professors receiving their first professional degrees from institutions in the Federal District (20 percent received their first degrees from UNAM). Other universities training significant numbers are Nuevo León (19 percent), San Luis Potosí (10 percent), the Technological Institute of Monterrey (9 percent), and Veracruz (7 percent). Thus, five institutions provided the first professional degrees for 65 percent of all professors in our sample. Only four professors (1 percent) were graduates of the National Polytechnic Institute.

There are a few important differences among professors teaching in the various types of faculties with respect to their first professional training, as indicated in Appendix Table 13. The prospective professor of science, engineering, or agronomy is apt to have crossed state boundaries in order to get his training in the state of Nuevo León (probably at the University of Nuevo León or the Technological Institute of Monterrey), while prospective professors of medicine, law, economics, and business administration are more apt to have attended their home universities. The fact that 15 percent of professors in the faculties of philosophy are foreign-trained may suggest that certain disciplines and specialties are just now becoming available in some of the Mexican universities.

The traditional five-year *licenciatura* programs in the faculties of law, economics, and philosophy and the six-year program in medicine are reflected in the summary of number of years of training by faculty type in Appendix Table 14. Greater variation exists in the training of professors of science, engineering, and agronomy, with a substantial percentage (35 percent) having only the four-year university bachelor's degree and an equal percentage (34 percent) holding masters, doctorates, and other higher certificates (see Appendix Table 15). It is probably more than coincidence that the pattern of training is least fixed precisely in the fields that have been most concerned with changing programs to meet new social and economic needs.

The principal sources of graduate training for the 132 professors in our sample of 327 who had proceeded beyond the professional degree are UNAM (17 percent), the Technological Institute of Monterrey (18 percent), and U.S. institutions (34 percent).[5]

Relatively heavy reliance seems to be placed on Monterrey for science, engineering, and business administration; on UNAM for medicine, engineering, and law; on El Colegio de México for economics; on the United States for medicine, science, and engineering; and on Europe for philosophy, science, and engineering (see Appendix Table 16).

Thus, in the provincial universities there is a relatively young group of professors. A number--

perhaps a third--of them have ventured on to graduate study, but the large majority, although still young, have not gone beyond the master's level or have not yet gone beyond their first professional degrees (see Appendix Tables 17 and 18).

Not surprisingly, a majority of the professors in our sample who went on to post-graduate education were to be found among the non-hourly (full-time and half-time) appointees. Of 164 non-hourly professors, 94 had taken study beyond their first degrees, while only 38 of 163 hourly professors had done so. Since we have purposely over-sampled full-time professors, the statistics on graduate study will show a higher proportion going on to further training than would be the case in the total population of professors. In terms of exposure of students to professors, however, the picture would be more nearly accurate since the full-time professors spend considerably more time in the university. In any case, the comparisons from field to field or university to university are generally valid since the sampling procedure is the same within each category.

The sources of graduate education for the hourly and non-hourly professors are as follows:

	Federal District	Nuevo León, Monterrey	Other Mexico	United States	Other Foreign	Number of Professors Reporting
Hourly	18%	42%	14%	8%	18%	38
Non-hourly	24%	16%	2%	45%	13%	94
						132

The influence of the two major institutions in the state of Nuevo León (the University of Nuevo León and the Technological Institute of Monterrey) in the graduate training of hourly professors is apparent, as is the importance of graduate training in the United States to full-time professors. Particularly noteworthy is the fact that over 20 percent of hourly professors and nearly 60 percent of non-hourly professors had undertaken graduate study, usually at institutions other than their own. These data belie another stereotype of the Latin American university professor--that of the practicing professional with little or no educational experience outside the first professional program of his home university. It further suggests that, as full-time appointments become more widely available and as university teaching careers become more attractive, students will be able to benefit from the much more varied educational experiences of professors. The full-time appointment seems to be worth the effort of post-graduate study.

Do professors go on to graduate training because there are well-established career incentives and recruiting and promotion procedures within and among institutions? The answer at the moment seems to be in the negative. Instead, encouragement toward graduate study seems to come through *ad hoc* fellowship and fellowship supplement programs from the home universities and through the availability of international fellowships, particularly in science and other development-related fields.

Recruitment

The data on geographical origins of provincial university professors (see Appendix Tables 10, 11, 12, 13, and 16) suggest that the norm is to teach in one's home university or to return to one's home university after pre-graduate or graduate training at UNAM or the major institutions in Monterrey. Apparently, mobility of professors among provincial universities is very low except among those with programs of graduate studies. It also appears that relatively little is done in the way of active recruitment of professors from one institution to another or even in the recruitment of prospective teachers in the graduate or professional programs of other institutions.

Interestingly, as became apparent during the pre-test of the questionnaire, there is no good Spanish or at least Mexican equivalent for the

English word "recruitment." The Spanish reclutamiento carries, at least in Mexico, a distinctly military connotation. Nombramiento, on the other hand, has more to do with the more formal process of appointment after the search is over. Contratación has much the same sense. The final somewhat laborious form of the question asked (in Spanish) whether there was "some system by which universities, prior to the contracting of professors, might discover through diverse sources who might be able to serve in the teaching faculty." Thirty-eight directors replied affirmatively. (A breakdown of their responses by faculty type and by four specific recruitment activities appears in Appendix Table 46.) Recruitment from among an institution's own graduates (and promotion from within) seems very much to be the rule, a finding that squares with the analysis of the source of professional training of professors. When universities do try to recruit from the outside, they do so through informal correspondence and visits. In adding other methods of recruitment, many of the respondents actually listed methods of selection (e.g., "exámen de oposición," "aprobación por el consejo técnico," "contratación por un año," and "examinación del curriculum vitae"). Apparently, not only is there no good term for "recruitment" but the very process itself does not play an important part in the development of teaching faculties and programs. Here, the stereotype of the inbred isolated faculty is partially confirmed.

When asked how they would improve the system of recruitment if they had more administrative funds available for the purpose, the deans who replied argued less for changes in procedures than for changes in incentives to professors.[6] One interesting reply was that, until better avenues of professional communication were opened (particularly through professional journals) and until professors came to be known in other universities through their published research, there probably would not be a great deal of professional mobility or professional advancement and individual promotion through change from one institution to another. Another cited the need to improve laboratories and equipment in order to attract better people. Others felt that programs of temporary exchange of professors would enhance more permanent recruitment from the outside. Still others felt that the present system of recruitment was adequate.

The rectors' responses confirmed the impression given by the directors' responses that the process of recruitment, as opposed to that of appointment, had not been given a great deal of attention. Only two of the six rectors indicated systematic efforts at recruitment, and they did so only in the categories suggested on the questionnaire itself (correspondence with other universities and professional associations, publicity in professional journals, and attempts to recruit the university's own best students). When asked how, with increased funds, they would improve the process of recruitment, the rectors replied that the problem was not recruitment _per se_ but the fact that more resources were needed for improved salaries for more full-time professors in order to attract people to the profession in the first place. Again, the need for a more appealing permanent professional career line in university teaching is apparent. Recruitment obviously would be easier if greater possibilities for advancement within the profession were established and made clear to candidates.

The process of appointment itself varies somewhat from university to university, and there are even variations within the same university. Yet basically it is quite similar both among faculties and among universities. Usually, a faculty committee screens candidates and makes nominations to the director, who makes the final decision himself (15 responses) or refers his own recommendation to the rector for a final decision (23 responses). Occasionally, the commission of professors or the _consejo técnico_ of the faculty make recommendations directly to the rector (14 responses). Finally, recommendations originated by a committee of professors may pass either through the rector or directly to the university council (9 responses). The quality of the appointee, of course, still depends on the quality of the candidates who compete for it.

Promotion and Development

Most deans (47) reported that there was no regular promotion system within their faculties. This fact was confirmed by the rectors' responses. A few deans reported a regular procedure within the faculty for reviewing, through an ad hoc committee, the performance and productivity of present members of the faculty with an eye toward appointments to higher rank; one reported that there was a system for merit promotion; and two reported that there was some variation in pay within rank. But in most instances, there was no variation in pay within rank and even the variation among ranks was somewhat more apparent than real, with many receiving the title of professor upon initial appointment. Consequently, most of the examples of "promotion" given were merely adjustments of hourly load, changes from hourly to full-time status, or automatic changes in pay according to years of service or other criteria specified by the General Law of the university. A few deans reported that the present system was being studied or that a commission was at work establishing personnel policy including a promotion system. In general, however, the initial appointment seems all-important. As indicated elsewhere in this chapter, there are certain incentives provided for self-improvement of professors. Yet even these incentives have more to do with defraying the cost of post-graduate study than with providing the basis for an orderly career advancement within the profession.

Thus, in the absence of the flow of a regular career progression, some of the vestiges of the colonial cátedra system remain--particularly the undue importance attached to the original appointment and the lack of promotion by merit.

Are the provincial universities systematically attempting to improve the quality of their teaching faculties? The answer seems clearly to be affirmative, with 41 of the 66 directors indicating that there was some sort of formal program for faculty improvement. Over half these programs were established prior to 1963, and they appear to be best established in faculties of engineering, agronomy, and economics.[7] Programs of self-improvement take numerous forms, but those most frequently cited by directors are round-table discussions and pedagogical in-service training within the university, fellowships and fellowship supplements for study at other universities, and provision for sending professors to summer and other short courses at UNAM, El Colegio de México, and the Technological Institute of Monterrey.[8] In general, these practices were confirmed by the rectors, who also made note of the use of visiting professors and lecturers and the support of regional and national congresses and symposia. Several also mentioned programs for the further development of the teachers in the <u>preparatoria</u> administered by the university. One rector described a new program for both scientists and humanists at the master's level organized by the university's council for scientific research. Long-range plans call for an extension of this program to the doctoral level.

If many of the incentives of an orderly long-term career progression still remain to be established in the provincial university, short-term encouragement for educational self-development is already actively at work. And so yet another stereotype--the professor whose development stops with his first professional degree--must be altered.

The formal and informal self-improvement of professors apparently includes a substantial amount of language training. Almost all professors in all fields but law and philosophy had some knowledge of English, with medical doctors expressing greatest confidence in their competence. In general, non-hourly professors expressed greater linguistic self-confidence than did hourly professors. At two of the universities, the Technological Institute of Monterrey and Sonora, virtually all professors in the sample reported a working knowledge of English. Because of the proximity of Mexican universities to the United States, the sample of language abilities undoubtedly is not representative of Latin American universities in general. In the universities of

Argentina and Chile, language competence in other European languages, particularly French and German, no doubt greatly exceeds the present relatively modest accomplishments in those languages reported by Mexican professors.[9] The relatively high common competence in even one foreign language has importance for instruction, as we shall see.

When asked how they keep up-to-date with their profession, approximately 90 percent of the professors in each field cited regular reading of journals and books in the field as most important. Conferences, seminars, and short courses were regarded as next most important, particularly by doctors, natural scientists, agronomists, and economists. The next most popular category, professional contacts and correspondence, was particularly favored by professors of philosophy. "Personal research," the third most popular response, was the special choice of lawyers.

The Mexican professor turns out to be a joiner of professional societies. Of our sample of 327 professors, 220 reported membership in at least one professional society, with 102 belonging to 2 or 3 and 38 belonging to more than 3.[10] Distribution by type of faculty is shown in Appendix Table 21. That membership in professional societies in Mexico implies some participation is confirmed by the fact that 175 of the 220 professors who were members of professional societies actually attended one or more meetings of their societies in 1967. Incidentally, the responses suggest that the societies function not merely as trade unions, as the stereotype suggests, but as organizations for the advancement of knowledge.

Professors were asked whether they undertook consulting jobs, and 102 of the 327 replied in the affirmative. It is conceivable that this item was not clearly interpreted as referring to an activity distinct from regular employment outside the university. Over 50 percent of the lawyers and over 33 percent of doctors, engineers, and economists report that they consult; about two-thirds of the consultations involve private organizations and one-third involve public agencies. Hourly and non-hourly professors report an approximately equal number of consultations.

In light of the rather considerable evidence of self-help in self-improvement and institutional policies of assistance to the individual in his efforts at self-development, it is surprising to find only 25 of 67 deans indicating any long-term economic incentives for post-graduate study.[11] The most common incentive was the possibility of moving from one rank to another or from hourly to full-time status. Since graduate study is not actually required for either form of advancement and since salary increases within grade are frequently not possible under the university law, a professor's drive for further education must be largely inner-directed.

In general, the rectors confirmed the lack of incentives other than those cited above, although two made the point that graduate study may be important in the appointment of department heads and directors of schools.

Both the professors themselves, in their descriptions of formal and informal attempts at continuing professional self-improvement,[12] and the rectors and directors, in describing institutional efforts to foster such professional development, seem to belie the stereotype of the stagnant professional university in which all professors are practitioners and all are graduates of the same program that they are now at pains to perpetuate. Continuing professional self-development is still far from a universal phenomenon, but it is apparently a much more common practice today than in the recent past.

THE LIBRARY

To what extent are the faculty and university administrations attempting to improve the resources that support teaching and research? The most critical resource would seem to be the library and its various services. A recent survey of university libraries in Mexico provides important information at the national level and analyzes responses from university officials, particularly professional librarians.[13] However, it seemed worthwhile to take advantage of the solicitation of information from directors and professors to get a more close-up view of the use of libraries, both departmental and central.

Although only one of the nine universities in the study apparently does not have a central library, only 47 of the 66 directors answered questions about the libraries at their universities. Eight left the questionnaire blank on the central library question, and an additional four were apparently under the impression that the university had no central library services when in fact it did.

Less than one-third of the directors indicated that the central library (1) provided professors with information about new books, translations, or periodicals, (2) made available reserve shelves for individual courses, (3) allowed books to circulate to students' homes, or (4) acquired books on recommendation from professors.[14] Apparently, these services are systematically provided in only three of the nine universities. Faculties of economics and business administration make fairly good use of the four services in question, but law schools make virtually none.[15]

The rectors' reports of the availability of central library services were far more positive than those of the directors, but the professors (see Appendix Table 33) tended to confirm the directors' opinions. Apparently, services are theoretically available but in practice they are either not requested or not provided.[16]

As is clear from Appendix Tables 33, 34, and 41, the faculty libraries play a much more important part in the instructional process than do central university libraries. An exception to this is the Technological Institute of Monterrey, where the reverse is true. In all, 58 of the 66 responding deans indicated that their schools did have their own libraries.

What are these faculty libraries like? In the first place they are very small. Only one faculty reported as many as 10,000 volumes and one had as few as 100. The median number of volumes was 1,300; 10 percent had fewer than 300 volumes; 30 percent fewer than 700; 70 percent fewer than 2,700; and 90 percent fewer than 5,000.

The median number of subscriptions to Spanish-language journals was 4, as was the number of subscriptions to non-Spanish journals. Six faculties reported no subscriptions to Spanish-language journals, while 10 faculties reported that they subscribed to no non-Spanish journals. (A complete breakdown of holdings by faculty type is presented in Appendix Table 40.) The figures, particularly the figures for journal subscriptions, low as they are, probably represent over-estimates since the 13 deans who did not report figures are more apt to represent faculties with small numbers of general subscriptions or none at all. All but one of Monterrey's deans reported that their faculties did not have libraries but used the central facility. Of the other universities, Sonora had the largest median holding of books for faculty libraries (3,200), the largest median number of Spanish-language journal subscriptions (9), and the largest median number of English-language journal subscriptions (14).

Although the faculty library holdings sometimes are no larger than those of a good personal library, reading space is somewhat more adequate if still limited. The average library reading space accommodates 40 persons, and 10 percent of the faculty libraries have room for 100 persons or more. Even the very smallest libraries (lowest 10 percent) tend to accommodate up to 15 persons. Thus, the largest libraries have room for almost as many persons as the smallest libraries have for books. The largest reading rooms are owned by medical faculties, with 4 out of 8 deans of medical faculties reporting reading accommodations for over 100 persons.

The circulation, reserve, and acquisition services, which seem to be available to fewer than one-quarter of the faculties from central libraries, are provided to a somewhat greater degree by the faculties' own libraries. However, some faculties are without such assistance from either source (see Appendix Table 41). Central and faculty libraries jointly do seem to respond to professors' requests, although budgets are severely limited (see below). The best acquisition service seems to be provided in faculties of medicine, engineering, economics, and philosophy. Except in law schools, fair coverage seems to be provided for "outside" circulation of books to students. Information on new publications seems to be very spotty except in faculties of engineering and economics. The practice and service of reserve shelves for individual courses seems to be found primarily in faculties of economics, engineering, and philosophy. Responses by professors by and large corroborate the deans' reports of available faculty library services (see Appendix Table 34). Of special note in the professors' sample is the fact that the medical school professors make virtually no use of central library services. Use of central library services by most other types of faculties also is minimal (see Appendix Table 33).

Although, according to deans, the faculty libraries provide twice the services that the central libraries provide (see Appendix Table 41), only one-third of the deans reported sums earmarked for acquisitions and these were modest in the extreme (see Appendix Table 42). The median budget for acquisitions in all faculty libraries is only $1,300, despite the fact that median budgets for faculties of medicine and agronomy exceed $4,000 per year. In relation to the services that they could theoretically provide, some of the central library budgets for acquisitions are even more restrictive (see Appendix Table 43). Several directors indicated that faculty libraries were dependent primarily on gifts for their acquisitions.

The typical faculty library (55 deans reporting) has a total of one full-time employee earning about $100 per month. Typically, she is a high school graduate (bachillerato) without formal training in library science and without university training (see Appendix Table 44). Scanty as the resources for acquisitions in the faculty libraries are, the low level of professional service available seems even more serious. Even though deans and professors draw more often (apparently twice as often) on faculty libraries than on central libraries for their teaching and research, it is clear that the librarian is viewed more as a clerk than as a professional--someone to mind the store and protect the existing holdings. Although this study does not attempt to survey the services of central libraries, a report by Carl M. White suggests that there, too, the problem of lack of professional service exceeds even the deficiencies in holdings. Of 220 university librarians surveyed, only 4 had library degrees, only 9 had university degrees of any sort, and only 53 had proceeded beyond the preparatoria.[17]

As the directors looked back over the preceding five years (see Appendix Table 45), they saw gains in their faculty libraries primarily in terms of increased acquisitions, improved cataloging, and improved physical facilities. Only one director noted as most significant the improvement in the training of library personnel. (Sixteen directors failed to respond.) Eleven directors saw either no gains or an actual deterioration.[18]

When asked about changes in the central libraries in the preceding five years, 40 directors failed to respond. Of the 26 who did reply, 9 disclaimed any knowledge of what had been happening in the central library and 6 said either that there had been no change or that there had actually been a deterioration of services. This left a total of 11 positive responses about changes in the central libraries, divided about equally among improvement in cataloging, improvement in the training of library personnel, increases in acquisitions, and physical improvements.

In looking to the future, most directors seek improvements in their libraries largely through increased acquisitions, improved cataloging, and better facilities. Only 10 percent listed the need for improved training of library personnel.[19]

Despite the obviously urgent need for increasing the holdings of faculty libraries and particularly the numbers of subscriptions to professional journals, the need for better personnel seems, if anything, even more urgent. It is entirely possible that more deans would have checked this latter need with a multiple-choice questionnaire. Yet, it seems even more significant that when deans were given complete freedom of response the need for professional training should have ranked behind the more tangible necessities.

The rectors viewed library changes and needs from a somewhat broader perspective. They made note of changes in procedure ("*incorporación de las técnicas y medidas de organización moderna para este tipo de Instituciones*"), reorganization of systems of circulation, new security measures, use of the library for training of secondary or even primary students, and better study arrangements. One rector saw a future possibility for opening small branch libraries of the university library in the *barriadas* of his city and providing service in surrounding rural areas through *unidades moviles*. Several mentioned new systems of documentation including microfilm. One rector was determined to improve relations between his university library and important national and international repositories toward the end, among others, of exchanging books and catalogs. One rector noted sadly that various expositions, lectures, and bibliographic publications had had to be suspended for lack of funds. Another echoed the feeling of financial uncertainty in looking at the future:

> No teniendo ninguna perspectiva próxima de mejoría en nuestros ingresos, no podemos planear nada al respecto.

If ideas are not lacking, financial support unfortunately is.

Perhaps the only area in which the negative stereotype of the traditional Latin American university holds in Mexico with all too accurate validity is that of library service. Three universities seem to have effective central libraries, but only one seems to use it to really good advantage. A relatively small number of faculty libraries in medicine and agronomy are operating with good effect. But the general picture is bleak, with few physical and human resources and with no effective demand from professors and students for improvement.

THE CLASSROOM

If, for reasons of funding or habit, the central and faculty libraries are not actively used in instruction, what can be said of the approaches to classroom instruction that *are* being used? Some of the harsher critics of the Latin American university have set a stereotype of a university classroom in which the *catedrático* (professor) delivers lectures prepared in past years while students dutifully record the ancient observations as he drones on. Sometimes, students have the opportunity to purchase his notes (*apuntes*) from him and are freed from the drudgery of note-taking. No outside reading, student commentary or criticism, or individual thoughts are sought or even welcomed or listened to.

Although a questionnaire is a relatively poor substitute for direct observation, our evidence indicates a far more balanced approach to instruction than the stereotype suggests. Only 40 percent of the 327 professors in our sample indicated that they provided students with prepared *apuntes*, and most of the reasons advanced for using *apuntes* were entirely plausible. The responses to the question of why *apuntes* were used instead of published texts seemed to fall into four groups. The most frequently cited set of reasons (46 percent of responses) has to do with the necessity of supplementing, adapting, or selecting from text material. The most common response within this category (over half the responses) was the need to simplify material from the texts being used. The next most cited set of reasons (42 percent) for using apuntes was that appropriate texts simply were not available. Primary complaints within this category were lack of good Spanish translations for the most modern texts and lack of texts that dealt with all the areas the professor wished to cover. Only 12 professors listed cost of texts as the reason for resorting to reproduced notes. A few suggested that notes were a good pedagogical exercise for students. Engineers seem to make heaviest use of apuntes, while natural scientists use them least (see Appendix Table 29). Non-hourly professors and professors at Monterrey and Veracruz seem not to favor this form of instructional method.[20]

Professors in provincial Mexican universities require their students to use textbooks regularly, and most of them assign outside reading as well.[21] Indeed, the majority of courses appear to be single textbook courses supplemented by apuntes or reference material. Appendix Tables 29 through 32 give a composite picture of the use of personal lecture notes, texts, reference books, and journals by professors. Law, economics, and medical professors, in particular, seem to make relatively heavy use of the single text (in Spanish) supplemented by one or two favorite reference books (also in Spanish) and an occasional journal in Spanish or, in the case of medicine, in English. Most extensive use of non-Spanish (usually English) language texts and reference books is made by professors in the natural science fields. Professors of law and philosophy make almost no use of non-Spanish texts, reference books, or journals. Non-hourly professors make greater use of all categories of non-Spanish publications. The sharpest contrast is in the use of non-Spanish journals: Fewer than 10 percent of hourly professors assigned readings in such journals while over one-third of non-hourly professors made such assignments.

There were no real surprises in the classroom methodologies employed by professors, perhaps because a questionnaire is so much less satisfactory a tool than direct observation. Somewhat over half the professors reported regularly using lectures (clase magistral), with the largest proportion found in the natural sciences (81 percent) and the smallest (25 percent) in philosophy. The method of exposición (roughly an explicación de texte) was equally popular and had special appeal to professors of law, with 71 percent using it regularly. Most popular is the discussion, which is used by roughly three-quarters of professors in all faculty types. In light of subsequent data on class size and in the relative absence of the practice of sectioning of courses, it seems doubtful that discussion is effective in very large classes. Research plays a regular part in the courses of 40 percent of the professors with over 60 percent of lawyers and philosophers and only 16 percent of agronomists so indicating. Obviously, research in law and philosophy on the one hand and agronomy on the other suggests quite different activities. Professors of law and philosophy make greater use of required essays (over 85 percent as compared to an overall average of 68 percent) and some of these essays undoubtedly are described as research. Virtually all professors of law and philosophy require reference notes and bibliographies, while only 75 percent of professors in other faculties do. An average assignment for the 50 percent of professors reporting is 2 essays per semester, each about 15 pages in length. The total number of pages per semester for essays and reports runs close to 40 in faculties of natural science and just over 20 in faculties of law and philosophy.

Another stereotype of instruction in Latin American universities, deriving in some large degree from Rudolph Atcon's perceptive but overly polemical work,[22] is that it is concerned with pouring undigested and often indigestible unrelated facts into the empty vessel that is the student. In response to an open-ended question asking their opinions on the relative importance of instructional methods, 169 of 327 professors took the trouble to answer. Approximately 40 percent of the replies were variations of the statement "it depends"; for example:

> Cada método se debe aplicar de acuerdo a la materia, alumnos y circunstancias.

However, an even greater proportion suggested that getting the student to think for himself and getting him to participate were the most important aims of instructional methodology.[23] Faculties of natural sciences and economics supported these later positions most frequently and those of medicine least often. Distribution of types of opinion among hourly and non-hourly professors was very similar.

Instructional method is, of course, related to time, numbers, hourly load, outside commitments, and available technology. This last issue is analyzed in some detail in a recent study of instructional technology in Mexican universities. Among that study's findings are the following:

> On almost every measure of presence or use of instructional aids, the Faculty of Law is the "poor daughter" of the Mexican university, which conforms to the stereotype on this matter throughout Latin America. Similarly, on almost all measures, Medicine is the favored faculty. Physical Sciences had the highest unit costs when the aggregate measure of budget per student was used; but this is a poor measure for analyzing cost and quality in universities.
>
> The duplicating machine is the most commonly encountered piece of equipment, according to the Directors of faculties and schools. The calculator is the least common. Teaching through T.V., even on open circuit, is still rare in Mexico. (The English version of this study reports much less data on individual schools than will the Spanish; but only five universities--Iberoamericana, Instituto Politécnico, Tecnológico de Monterrey, UNAM and Tamaulipas--reported the use of instructional T.V.) Arrangements of instruction through joint courses and visiting lecturers is rare in faculties of humanities and law and more common in physical sciences and economics. There are significant differences in pos-

session of teaching aids according to the kind of faculty or school, except on very rare or very common items which most schools have, or few schools have. Static displays (maps, charts and wall displays) are the common instructional aids which all faculties have. Computers and T.V.'s are rarely owned by any faculty. In general, however, faculties have very few teaching aids of any kind.

Professors reported that they most wanted film strip projectors and opaque projectors. Much of the acquisition of teaching aids, however, does not depend on action within the faculty or school or by the Director. One fifth of the aids come to the faculty through donations; one third are purchased centrally in the university and allocated to the faculty.[24]

INSTRUCTIONAL LOAD

It is our purpose to examine here the professor's teaching, laboratory, and advising loads. The professor's outside commitments are examined in the following section.

On the basis of the professors' own reports of teaching hours,[25] we find that the typical (median) class is offered 3 hours per week, although the number of class hours in law, engineering, and particularly medicine exceed that median figure (see Appendix Tables 22 and 23). Medical school laboratory sessions also tend to be longer than those in other faculties (averaging approximately 4 hours per week), no doubt reflecting the clinical nature of the exercise. Class hours per course per week for hourly and non-hourly professors seem to be essentially equivalent.

Our questionnaire posed a problem for the estimation of total teaching load for individual professors in that the majority of professors did not indicate whether the courses they listed were semester courses or full-year courses. With the help of general catalog information and information on general policy within particular universities provided from ANUIES records, each course listed was coded according to the best estimate of whether it was for a semester or a full year. (Simple addition of course hours, if some are not annual courses, of course produces an over-estimate of teaching load at any one point in time.) Our best estimate was that over 60 percent of listed courses were, in fact, annual. (When there was real doubt, courses were coded as semester rather than full-year courses.) The hours for the semester courses were cut in half to arrive at the best estimate of actual teaching load.

The adjusted median class load per professor is approximately 10 hours per week, or roughly 3 courses per term. Twenty percent of all professors teach 15 or more hours per week. Although class loads appear to be heaviest in schools of law, the total number of contact hours for professors in schools of medicine and natural sciences is actually greater because of the supervision of laboratory sessions in addition to classroom instruction (see Appendix Tables 24 and 25). The average professor of medicine teaches a combined total of approximately 15 class and laboratory hours per week, while the professor of natural science teaches about 14. Hourly professors teach an average of 8 hours of classes per week; non-hourly professors teach about 12 hours per week. Although only 50 hourly as compared to 93 non-hourly professors conduct laboratory sessions, the average load is roughly equal--6 hours per week.

Although hours of teaching and laboratory commitments and administrative obligations provide one set of measures of the professor's teaching load, it is also necessary to look at the size of his classes and the total number of students he must instruct (see Appendix Table 26). Classes in the Mexican universities, even in the smaller universities, tend to be quite large. As was expected, since enrollments are greater in the earlier years, our random sample picked up professors teaching a larger percentage of classes in the earlier years than in the later years (see Appendix Table 27). The figures on class size reported in Appendix Table 28 should be read in comparison with Appendix Table 26. Law faculties have the largest classes overall (a median enrollment of 52 for 100 classes reporting), but medicine is close behind with a median of 47 and has the largest number of very large classes--10 percent of all classes in medicine are over 160 students. Philosophy has far and away the smallest median class size (15). Philosophy, natural sciences, and engineering have the largest number of very small classes (10 percent of the classes in these 3 fields are below 7, 6, and 13 persons, respectively).

The total number of students taught by each professor each week varies by type of faculty. Law professors have much the heaviest load with a median figure of 160 students per professor per week as compared to an overall median of about 100. Twenty percent of the law professors teach 240 or more students per week (see Appendix Table 26). Lowest student loads are to be found in faculties of philosophy, which often include specialized programs in journalism, modern foreign languages, and social science. The average hourly professor teaches about 80 students per week; the average non-hourly professor teaches about 120 students per week.

The average professor in all faculties except law reports that, in addition to his teaching and laboratory supervision, he spends 9 to 14 hours per week in <u>asesoría</u>. That is to say, he is available for consultation or has office hours 9 to 14 hours per week. The average law school professor is available about 3 hours per week for consultation with students. Hourly professors report an average of 5 to 6 hours per week of consultations with students, while non-hourly professors report over twice that many.

Almost half the professors in our sample reported other appointments within the university in addition to their primary teaching assignments.[26]

Those who do have secondary appointments spend a median of 11 hours per week at the job, although 20 percent spend 24 hours or more per week. The secondary appointment is a phenomenon common to each type of faculty; the variations among faculties in percentage of professors holding such appointments and the number of hours they spend on the second job are not significant. Predictably, the number of non-hourly professors holding secondary jobs inside the university (72) exceeds the number of hourly professors so employed (40).

Assistants are sometimes provided for professors who have to teach very large classes.[27] Almost one-quarter of classes reported by professors have at least one assistant. The grand total of assistants reported by the 327 professors in our sample is 324. However, almost 300 of these are provided in the science fields and are, apparently, laboratory assistants. Some 145 are to be found in the field of medical teaching and laboratory work, 68 in the natural sciences, 68 in engineering, and 16 in agronomy.

The Mexican professor thus carries an average weekly load of 3 courses, 10 hours of classes, and 100 students with relatively little assistance. (Laboratory work in addition to this load does carry with it some assistance.) And he carries not only a relatively heavy academic load inside the university but also a substantial outside load.

OUTSIDE COMMITMENTS

Seventy-eight percent (121) of the hourly professors and 40 percent (64) of the non-hourly professors report employment outside the university. About one-third of the jobs for both hourly and non-hourly professors are in teaching. These are mainly at the university (professional) level, although 7 professors teach at the preparatory and 3 at the junior high school level. Most non-teaching employment is in the practice of the man's own profession (87 cases), with administrative work within his professional field next most common (26 cases). Thirty-five professors held at least two jobs outside the university.

The 121 hourly professors who have outside jobs devote an average of 25 hours per week to this employment. Although this is a very substantial amount of time, it does not quite correspond to the stereotype of the hourly professor who works 40 hours per week at his regular job and spends a few evening hours in an honorific role as professor. Both the hourly professors who hold outside jobs and the 40 who earn their living entirely from the university are undoubtedly economically dependent on their university positions.

The outside commitment of the 64 full-time professors who do not work exclusively for the university is surprisingly modest, averaging as it does only 10 hours per week. Nevertheless, the total weekly load (teaching and non-teaching) does mount up. Of the 164 non-hourly professors, 55 list specific commitments totaling 40 hours or more per week (apart from reading, research, and class preparation), and 71 of the hourly professors have schedules that are equally crowded. Fifty-two non-hourly professors and 23 hourly professors list specific commitments totaling 30 to 39 hours per week. The professor in the Mexican provincial university does not appear undercommitted to his university. If anything, he is badly overcommitted to specific obligations both inside and outside his university. Clearly, he has all too little opportunity to read, write, think, and do research.

The high proportion of hourly professors in Mexican universities (85 percent) and the freedom accorded to full-time professors (except those appointed on _tiempo exclusivo_) to hold outside employment has suggested to outside observers a lack of commitment to university affairs. The evidence thus far cited seems to contradict this view. So too does the evidence about permanence of employment. Of the 222 professors who listed their university jobs in the preceding 5 years, almost half (101, or 46 percent) were able to say that they had held essentially the same job; 54 (24 percent) had held two jobs; and 67 (30 percent) had held 3 or more jobs. Thirty reported having been in the same primary job for 9 or more years and 70 indicated a period of 5 to 8 years. The other 102 professors were divided equally among 1, 2, 3, and 4 years of service. Many of those with the shorter periods of service, of course, are the young recent graduates who comprise the teaching staffs of most of the provincial universities.

Job stability is approximately equal among faculty types, although the percentage of medical doctors holding a single primary job for the preceding 5 years was 37 percent, well below the average of 46 percent. Engineers appear to have the most stable employment: Only 17 percent had had 3 or more jobs in the preceding 5 years. Economists and business administrators show the largest percentage (20 percent) holding jobs for 9 or more years. Interestingly, the number of jobs and the number of years per job were very nearly the same for hourly and non-hourly professors. The universities with the largest percentage of professors with 7 or more years of continuous service (Guadalajara and the Technological Institute of Monterrey) are also the universities with the oldest faculty members in the sample.

All in all, the picture of employment suggests less turnover and greater stability than might have been anticipated. Those who hold full-time appointments apparently regard university teaching as a permanent career. Since there is apparently not the same geographical mobility in the academic labor market as in the United States, full-time professors continue to remain full-time professors at the same university. As we have seen, even the full-time professor is apt to hold jobs outside the university. It is conceivable, even probable, that these outside jobs tend to reduce geographical mobility. It is hard enough to arrange for one new job; to arrange for two or more new ones in the same location is considerably more difficult. The same reasoning applies to the part-time professor, probably with even greater force.

Despite quite remarkable continuing efforts of individual professors to improve themselves (aided occasionally by _ad hoc_ programs of support from university administrations) and despite the professors' efforts to create for themselves a regular permanent profession through increasing commitment of time and energy to the university, it seems clear that the university has been financially and administratively unable to provide the necessary incentives of salary, full-time appointment, library and laboratory facilities, and research support. For the same reason, the university is greatly handicapped in its efforts to respond to and create change in provincial society, although evidence of such change is apparent in the newer scientific and economic professions. The very fact that it is still so easy to categorize all of higher education into seven professional families, as we have done in this book, suggests the relative sluggishness of the traditional nineteenth-century professional university in producing fundamental internal change and in increasing the diversity of its educational aims and methods.

NOTES

1. _La Educación Superior en México, 1967_ (México: ANUIES, 1969).

2. Social Progress Trust Fund, _Socio-Economic Progress in Latin America_, Seventh Annual Report (Washington, D.C.: Inter-American Development Bank, 1968), p. 328.

3. _La Educación Superior en México, 1967_, _op. cit._, p. 196.

4. There is relatively little variation in the median age of professors among the samples from the nine universities studied. Interestingly enough, the sample from Nuevo León, one of the largest universities, was the only one not to include any professors who had completed _preparatoria_ prior to 1940, while Veracruz, another of the largest, had the smallest percentage of professors completing

preparatoria prior to 1950. The median year of graduation from *preparatoria* for hourly teachers was 1954, while the median for non-hourly (full- and half-time) professors was 1952. (For F test among faculty types, $p = .001$; among universities, $p = .18$.)

5. Of the 132 professors from our sample of 327 who had done some sort of graduate study, 29 (22 percent) pursued their studies in the Federal District, 32 (24 percent) in the state of Nuevo León, and 45 (34 percent) in the United States. Twenty-six of these last 45 were professors at the Technological Institute of Monterrey. The two institutions at which the largest number of Mexican professors in our sample did their graduate study are UNAM (23 individuals, or 17 percent) and the Technological Institute of Monterrey (24 individuals, or 18 percent). The two regions in the United States that were most popular for graduate study were the northeast and the north central; in each of these regions, 13 individuals in our sample had done their graduate study.

6. Twelve suggested various kinds of incentives to encourage the post-graduate training of present faculty members or graduating students, and 8 suggested that more full-time appointments and better salary scales would be necessary in order to recruit from other universities. Five deans spoke of better methods of selection, and 5 others felt that with additional funds some division of labor could be effected to reduce the teaching loads of senior professors and give them more time to assist in recruiting.

7. Three-fourths or more of faculties of engineering, agronomy, and economics had programs for the upgrading of professors, while less than 50 percent of faculties of medicine and philosophy had such programs. The only university with more than 75 percent of its directors reporting such programs was the Technological Institute of Monterrey, with 100 percent. In general, policies supporting professors in their efforts to improve their professional skills are fairly long-established, with half of them antedating 1963 and 17 established before 1960. (For F test among faculty types, $p = .18$--not

significant; among universities, $p = .60$--not significant.)

8. According to the directors, the nature of the faculty improvement programs is quite varied. Most typical (cited by 13 of 67 directors) is some sort of in-service pedagogical and professional training or a system of round-table discussions within the university; equally popular is support for formal post-graduate study through a regular or supplementary fellowship fund of the universities or through provision for released time within the same university (13); next most typical is provision for sending professors to summer courses or other short courses in other Mexican institutions, particularly UNAM, El Colegio de México, and the Technological Institute of Monterrey (10); and other faculty improvement programs include international funds regularly available for graduate study (2), special courses offered by visiting professors (1), and the "incentive" of competitive examination and review (oposición) for promotion (2).

Of our sample of 327 professors, 170 reported that they were involved in self-development programs supported to some degree by their own faculties or universities. Of these, 72 were in schools of economics and business administration. Among universities, Veracruz seemed to have the most active program of support, with 40 professors reported to be receiving benefits. Next most active were the Technological Institute of Monterrey (25), Nuevo León (24), Guadalajara (22), and Estado de México (21).

9. Of our sample of 327 professors, 285 reported knowing a second language, with 271 indicating that their best second language was English while only 7 indicated French. Of the 285, 140 reported that they could read, write, and speak well, 62 fairly well, and the rest just enough to get along. Some 128 reported knowing a second foreign language (90 indicated French and 18 Italian), but only 34 claimed to know the second language well. Fifty-four indicated an acquaintance with a third language--Portuguese (8) and German (11) now begin to appear--

but only 12 claimed any sort of mastery. One professor claimed a knowledge of 9 languages.

Of 56 doctors and dentists in the sample, 49 indicated a knowledge of English, as did 42 of 43 natural scientists, 67 of 73 engineers, 24 of 24 agronomists, 56 of 70 economists and business specialists, 14 of 31 lawyers, and 19 of 28 professors in faculties of philosophy. The doctors and dentists were most confident about their abilities in foreign language--66 percent said that they read, wrote, and spoke the language well--while only 33 percent of the lawyers reporting competence in a foreign language indicated an equal level of proficiency. Half the professors in other faculties who indicated knowledge of a foreign language rated themselves "competent" in it. Eighty-seven (58 percent) of the 149 non-hourly professors with knowledge of a second language said they knew it well, while only 65 (48 percent) of the 135 hourly professors rated themselves as high.

There was some variation in language competence among universities with virtually all professors at the Technological Institute of Monterrey and Sonora reporting a knowledge of English, 77 percent of the former and 67 percent of the latter indicating good mastery. Professors at San Luis Potosí (67 percent) and Nuevo León (67 percent) were also confident of their foreign language ability while the figures at Guanajuato (35 percent) and Veracruz (32 percent) were more modest. (For F test among faculty types on English fluency, p = .014; among universities, p = .000.)

10. Non-hourly professors were somewhat more "involved" professionally, with 116 memberships in professional societies while hourly professors had 104. The Technological Institute of Monterrey and Nuevo León, each with 40, had the largest number of memberships in professional societies, with San Luis Potosí (28) and Guadalajara (27) next in line. (For F test among faculty types, p = .000--see Appendix Table 21; among universities, p = .78--not significant.)

Hourly professors were almost as faithful in attendance at meetings of professional societies as non-hourly professors (86 to 89), with 20 percent of each group attending 2 or 3 meetings and 10 percent attending 4 or more. The most active participants were doctors (82 percent attending), followed by agronomists (60 percent), natural scientists (56 percent), lawyers (55 percent), engineers (48 percent), economists (41 percent), and philosophers (25 percent). Most active participants were to be found in the universities of Guadalajara, Estado de México, and Nuevo León. (For F test among faculties, $p = .07$; among universities, $p = .02$.)

11. In addition to enrolling in degree programs, a number of professors (111) attempted to upgrade themselves through non-degree work. The most typical method (81 cases) was for the professor to take a regular course in his own field, although internships (9 responses), _cursillos_ or short courses (11 responses), seminars (5 responses), and summer school (only 4 responses) also were cited. In addition to study in the professor's own field (71 responses), the study of languages (16), related fields (9), pedagogy (9), and computing (5) were most popular. Lawyers seemed to be relatively the most active in non-degree programs of self-development, perhaps because of the lack of higher-degree programs. Among the universities, Estado de México apparently had a higher proportion of professors engaging in this category of activities, perhaps because of the proximity of UNAM.

12. When asked whether economic incentives had been offered to professors who undertook post-graduate work, only 25 deans responded affirmatively. Thirteen cited the possibility of promotion from one grade to another or from an hourly to a full-time appointment or, less frequently, "a better position" within a given teaching category; 9 indicated rewards in terms of support for further study; and only 2 suggested salary increases as a possible _quid pro quo_.

13. Carl M. White, Mexico's Library and Information Services: A Study of Present Conditions and Needs (Totowa, N.J.: Bedminster, 1969).

14. Directors were asked whether their university's central library provided information to deans and professors about new books, periodicals, and translations (17 affirmative), whether it provided reserve shelves for individual courses (9 affirmative), whether it permitted books to circulate to the homes of students (16 affirmative), and whether it acquired books on recommendation from professors (21 affirmative).

15. The universities whose deans responded most often in the affirmative to questions on library services were the Technological Institute of Monterrey with 17 of a possible 20 positive responses, Veracruz (19/40), and Guanajuato (10/24). Only one other university showed as many as 6 affirmative responses to the 4 questions, suggesting that the practices investigated were in vogue in only 3 of the 9 universities. Faculties of economics and business administration used the 4 questioned services of the central library most, with 20 positive out of a total of 44 possible responses, while law schools used them least--one positive response out of a possible total of 28. (For F test among faculty types, $p = .184$--not significant; among universities, $p = .000$.)

16. Other central library services noted by the directors themselves included general service to and coordination with the departmental library (4); microfilm and copying service (3); bibliographic searches on particular themes (1); acquisition of books for special seminars (1); sale of books (1); and maintenance of a reading room (1).

Only 16 of the 66 directors indicated that their central libraries had subscriptions to professional journals of interest to them. This practice seemed to vary little among types of faculties but did show considerable variation among universities with 5/5 positive responses from the Technological Institute of Monterrey, 5/10 from Veracruz, 2/6 from Guanajuato, and no more than one positive response in any other university. Clearly, the responses depended more on the practices of particular central libraries than on the practices in particular types of faculties. All faculties listing 9 or more journals used from the central collection were to be found at the Technological Institute of Monterrey and Veracruz. (For F tests among faculties, p = .735--not significant; among universities, p = .000.)

Of the 59 professors reporting that their central libraries afforded them systematic information about new publications, 25 were at the Technological Institute of Monterrey, 12 at Veracruz, and 8 at Guanajuato. Of the 121 professors reporting similar services from their faculty libraries, most responses came from Veracruz (29), Nuevo León (19), Sonora (19), and Guanajuato (18). Of the 80 professors reporting that their central libraries cooperated in ordering books, most came from the Technological Institute of Monterrey (35), Veracruz (10), Guadalajara (9), and Guanajuato (8). Of the 67 professors reporting use of central library reserve shelves for their courses, the largest number of responses came from the Technological Institute of Monterrey (35), Veracruz (8), and Guanajuato (8).

17. White, op. cit., Table 32.

18. Fifty directors comment (71 responses) on changes in the faculty libraries. Eleven directors see no change or a deterioration in library services while principal gains are seen in increase in acquisitions (20 responses), improvement in cataloging (16), and physical improvements (13), including everything from furniture to air conditioning to new buildings.

19. When asked about the most pressing future needs for their own faculty libraries, 53 directors responded with a total of 83 observations. They saw the primary needs as increased acquisitions (37 responses), physical improvements (13 responses), and improvement in cataloging (13 responses). Only

8 responses (10 percent of total responses) referred to the need for improved training of library personnel. (Two responses saw no need for any improvements in faculty libraries.)

20. The heaviest use of apuntes occurred among professors of engineering (56 percent made regular use of apuntes), while professors of natural science (26 percent) made least use of them (see Appendix Table 29). Hourly professors (47 percent) were somewhat more prone to make regular use of apuntes than were non-hourly professors (34 percent). Professors at the universities of Guanajuato (66 percent) and Sonora (62 percent) made heaviest use of apuntes, while those at the Technological Institute of Monterrey (26 percent) and Veracruz (32 percent) used them least. (For F test among faculties, $p = .011$; among universities, $p = .014$.)

21. Of our sample of 327 professors, 70 indicated that they did not regularly require use of textbooks in their courses. The 70 are distributed about equally across types of faculty and between hourly and non-hourly professors. About three-fourths of the professors at each university indicated that they required the use of textbooks, except at the Technological Institute of Monterrey, where the figure was 96 percent. The number of required texts used per class is very small, the median being one Spanish-language text per course and one-third of a text in another language (that is, a non-Spanish text is used in one-third of the classes). About 10 percent of all professors use as many as 3 Spanish-language texts per course, while 16 percent of the professors use one or more non-Spanish texts per course. Virtually all professors require outside reading of their students.

22. Rudolph Atcon, The Latin American University (Bogotá: Editorial ABC, 1966).

23. Typical statements in support of various methods of instruction include the following: "Enseña a fijar su criterio," "Fomenta aprendizaje," "Favorece inquietud y libertad de criterio," "Motiva

y obliga a aprender sobre el trabajo práctico," "Activa participación directa de los alumnos," "Amplian el tema y facilitan al estudiante para discutirlo," or, somewhat cryptically, "Es necesario incrementar el diálogo entre maestros y alumnos y demostrar obselescencia de planes de estudio."

24. Noel F. McGinn (with Russell G. Davis and Richard G. King), The Technology of Instruction in Mexican Universities (New York: Education and World Affairs, 1968), p. 1.

25. One-quarter of the classes in medicine are over 7 hours per week and one in 10 is 12 hours per week or more. Laboratory schedules in medical schools are equally long, with the average weekly laboratory requirement in laboratory courses averaging 4 hours but extending to 7 or more in one-fourth of such courses and to 10 hours or more in one-tenth of the courses. The latter no doubt have to do with clinical instruction. Class hours per course per week reported by hourly professors are virtually identical to those reported by non-hourly professors, although laboratory courses are conducted by a few more non-hourly (63) than hourly (41) professors.

26. Seventy-two professors in our sample (22 percent) hold some sort of administrative position at the faculty level, and 7 (2 percent) hold administrative appointments at the university level. Twenty-three (7 percent) have research appointments; 20 (6 percent) do work for the university in their professional specialty; 20 (6 percent) work as counselors or members of special committees; and one is also an athletic coach.

27. Hourly and non-hourly professors have classes of about the same size, although the non-hourly professors have a few more very large classes of over 80 persons (30 non-hourly and 17 hourly professors reported having such classes) and also a few more very small classes of 15 persons and under (22 non-hourly and 15 hourly professors reported having such classes). Only 10 percent of all classes have 18 persons or less and only 5 percent of all classes

have 100 or more students. Forty percent of classes are at the awkward size (40 to 80), too large for discussion but not as large as they could be for a straight lecture presentation.

CHAPTER

5

ADMINISTRATIVE SUPPORT

The ability of an institution to respond to the social and economic needs of its region and improve its capacity for up-to-date, effective instruction is, of course, dependent in some large part on the administrative support that it can give to its instructional program. Here, we examine some elements of that support and some of the obstacles to improved administrative service. Particular attention will be given to improvements and constraints in matters of budgeting, finance, planning, and the administration of student affairs.

THE BUDGET

To what extent do the internal processes of decision-making aid or impede efforts toward change? On the assumption that educational decisions require budgetary support, both directors and rectors were asked about the budgetary process. In answer to the question of how the university's budget as a whole is determined, the six responding rectors, all from public state institutions, indicated some interesting procedural, political, and even philosophical differences. In three of the responding universities, the university council "sets" the budget. Unfortunately, the question did not elicit a description of the process of negotiation between university and state. Two of the six universities now have patronatos or boards of trustees which, although they do not have direct control of state and federal sources of funds, act to some degree as negotiating agents. Another rector responded that the budget is determined by the "junta de gobierno" according to "nuevas necesidades" and not on a fixed formula for state and federal funds. He said:

> No tenemos fijado ningún porcentaje de aumento automático, sino que estamos a expensas de lo que el Poder Estatal y Federal quieran aportar.

Probably, this response more adequately describes the process of the majority of the state universities. None of the directors describe a process of budgetary planning and negotiation that extends more than a year into the future.

The rectors stated that the internal distribution of the budget among faculties is a responsibility of the university council upon recommendation of the central administration, according to the needs of each faculty:

> De acuerdo a las necesidades planteadas por cada dependencia. . . .

> Tomando en cuenta el volumen de población escolar, las condiciones de trabajo de profesores y la situación de bibliotecas, laboratorios, etc.

Unfortunately, it is not clear how these determinations of need are made and according to what criteria. The impression remains that it is a year-to-year process of adjudicating competing claims of individual faculties rather than a longer-range process of planning according to program aims, particularly aims that cross faculty lines. One rector did indicate that final figures were determined "according to studies previously carried out by the budget commission of the university council."

Although rectors are principally impressed with evidence of increased enrollments in the various faculties in deciding on budgets, most also are preoccupied with improving the teaching faculty in all fields, improving general library and laboratory resources, and giving additional stimulus to research and programs of "cultural diffusion." However, one again gains the impression that the two most important factors in setting budgets are the differing rates of growth of the student population among faculties and the comparison with last year's budget ("la comparación de presupuestos del año en curso y para el que se va a presupuestar"). No mention is made of program goals or the evaluation of same as part of the budgetary process.

In answer to a question about changes in the budgetary system, rectors referred only to increases or decreases in the university's overall budget or to new more mechanized systems of budgetary control and financial (not program) audit. In answer to questions about improving the budgetary system, responses again generally were related to improving the accounting system or increasing resources. Apparently, it is difficult enough to get real control of the figures necessary for a clear financial audit. Clearly, it is not possible under present procedures to relate expenditures to instructional objectives in a program audit.

When deans were asked about the budgetary system, there was less than complete agreement within a given university as to exactly how the process of budgetary proposal and authoritative response actually operated. Although there are varying lines of authority in determining internal distribution of the budget, the final authority usually is the university council or the rector. It seems clear that, with the apparent exception of the University of Sonora, final budgetary authority for distribution of funds among faculties rests within the university.[1]

Most deans feel that the relative merits of the stated needs of individual faculties are weighed before final decisions are made on the allocation of funds among faculties, but 21 of our group of 66 feel that such is not the case. Greatest unanimity on the statement that appropriate consideration is given to individual faculty needs before allocation decisions are made seems to exist among faculties of engineering and architecture, and, among universities, in Veracruzana.

Directors generally agreed (36 of 53 responses) that the allocation of funds within faculties is made by the dean, according to a rational examination of the number of students, teaching hours, and physical needs for each program. The rector, treasurer, and trustees frequently share the responsibility. A few directors stated, that, if a fixed quota was not at work, present allocation of funds was primarily dependent on that of the previous year.[2] One-fourth of the directors indicated that professors participate in a substantial way in the preparation of the request budget in the first place.[3]

But neither at the faculty level nor at the university level is there an indication of a move toward program budgeting--the setting of general instructional or research goals and the use of the budget to define the resources needed to attain them. There is indication of required accountability, but the accountability is more for funds than for the realization of goals.

The directors viewed changes in the budgetary system over the preceding five years as changes in amount and extent rather than changes in kind or process. Principally noted were budgetary revisions to accommodate increases in enrollment, the addition of new _carreras_, and changes in salary schedules.[4] The most interesting response is that of 8 directors who replied that changes in certain administrative and personnel procedures were coming about through changes in the budgetary process. This development seems to be an important step toward the use of the budget to implement fundamental changes in the program rather than merely to add new _carreras_.

When asked whether the present budgetary system seemed acceptable, only 35 directors responded and 26 of them responded negatively. Judging from the nature of the earlier responses, the apparent lack of interest in the question stems from the view that the budget is just an administrative necessity rather than a process of communication (a process of proposal and response) and a potential device for marshaling resources in support of middle- or long-range goals. If the questionnaire had included questions on elements of program budgeting, the results might have been more satisfying. Nevertheless, the open-ended response seems to better describe the real views of budgeting held by directors.

What proposals would directors make for changing the budgetary system? It is not surprising that the problem uppermost in the deans' minds (16 of 41 total responses) was greater authority and freedom to manage the internal affairs of their faculties. Sample responses include the following:

> Que se atendiera a las opiniones de los directors.
>
> La función del patronato debe limitarse.
>
> Mas responsabilidad al propio consejo técnico de la escuela.
>
> Que se dejara a los Patronos solamente la determinación de presupuesto global y su distribución de hiciera por la dirección de la universidad y de las escuelas.
>
> Será deseable contar con presupuestos separados por escuelas independientemente de las areas comunes.
>
> Que estuviera ajustado a la realidad, de acuerdo con las necesidades de cada institución (escuela).
>
> Manejo de los fondos por un patrimonio de la misma, dando a cada escuela de acuerdo con sus necesidades.

> [Attention should be paid to the opinions of the directors.
>
> The functions of the board of trustees should be limited.
>
> More responsibility (should be given) to the technical council of the school.
>
> Only the determination of the total budget should be left to the trustees while its distribution should be made by the officers of the university and those of the separate schools.
>
> It would be desirable to have separate budgets for each school, independent of the areas of joint control.
>
> The budget should be adjusted to reality in accordance with the special needs of each school.
>
> The management of funds for a separate school should be in the hands of its own board of trustees so that the special needs of each school may be recognized.]

The sense of frustration is as clear as the sense of need for financial support. The latter feeling came out particularly in the responses of the 9 directors who said that what is wrong with the budgetary system is simply lack of funds.

The replies that were more responsive to the issue of process and system included the statement (4 responses) that priorities should be set and budgets determined by competent authorities who are, above all, impartial:

> El presupuesto aprobado sea fruto de la labor de un conjunto de autoridades representatives competentes e imparciales.
>
> Que la universidad realizara una investigación de las necesidades de cada depen-

> dencia jerarquizando las necesidades, un análysis mas profundo e imparcial de las necesidades.
>
> [The final budget should be the fruit of the labor of a team of representative, competent, and impartial authorities.
>
> The university should undertake an investigation of the needs of each school, setting priorities through a more thorough and more impartial analysis.]

Other responses related to process and system were: that budgets should reflect important new technical instructional needs (3 responses); that new kinds of research needs must be taken into account (2); that the budget must permit the planning of new activities 5 or 10 years into the future (2); that incentives for the self-improvement of professors need to be introduced into the budgetary system (1); and finally, and perhaps most interesting of all, that through the budgetary system the provincial universities must begin cooperatively to compete with the Federal District. One director stated:

> Cambios presupuestales de hacer una mejor distribución del presupuesto para la enseñanza superior en la provincia; evitar la creación innecesaria de nuevas instituciones; una buena regionalización de la enseñanza; disminuir el centralismo efectuando fuga de valores de provincia hacia la capital.
>
> [(There is need for) budgetary change to effect a more favorable allocation for higher education in the provinces; (it is important) to avoid the creation of new institutions that unnecessarily duplicate existing ones; (we need) an effective regionalization of instruction; (we need to) reduce centralism and the consequent flight of talent from the provinces to the capital.]

The need for administrative and programmatic change is clearly expressed in many of the replies, and there is a recognition that the budgetary process must play some role in such change. The policies, procedures, and techniques that will facilitate change are less clearly expressed.

FINANCE

The leitmotivs running through all discussions of budget are much more size and amount than procedure and process; the preoccupation is with financing rather than with budgeting. When asked if financing has kept pace with growth in enrollments, rectors with one exception replied in the negative, noting that federal subsidies had been very sluggish, particularly in the 1960s. However, all but one of the rectors indicated that new sources of funding for their universities had opened up in the preceding five years. At both the university and faculty levels, efforts had been made to create private _patronatos_ for purposes of fund-raising but not control. Some rectors noted new income from publications, musical and theatrical performances, and special grants from private philanthropic organizations. But the total amounts of private support are still very small. In the rectors' speculations about future sources of income, the most common suggestion was a substantial increase in tuition and fees coupled with a more active scholarship and loan program. Past efforts in this direction resulted in student strikes, but the rectors apparently feel that, with adequate attention to needy students, increases can and should come. With fees now set at $10 to $20 per student per year, this would seem to be a very reasonable suggestion.

The federal government is looked upon as the next most likely source of additional funding. Other suggestions include the previously mentioned _patronatos_, special taxes on university graduates who are practicing their professions, special taxes on gasoline or electricity, and even raffles and lotteries. Voluntary alumni giving is well down the list of possibilities.

According to the rectors, the chief obstacles to the opening of important new sources of funding have been "unjustified student protest" and lack of understanding on the part of businessmen and state, particularly federal, officials as to what the universities wish to do. As one rector admitted, the universities' interests have been hurt by lack of serious planning by the universities and lack of careful explanation of plans to the public.[5]

PLANNING

Planning means very different things in the various universities in our sample, according to rectors. Most typically, it is simply the annual budgetary process supplemented by a narrative report of activities.[6] In several cases, however, either there is a standing university committee for planning or planning is carried out by an _ad hoc_ commission, by the faculty of economics, or by one of the university's research institutes. Typically, these are incipient activities and finished planning documents were not available at the time of the survey.

The rectors indicated that the studies under way were to take account of both social and economic demand (projected) and that they were attempting to establish guidelines for maximum faculty loads. When asked if the university had established any normative student-faculty ratios, the 3 rectors who responded did so not in terms of such a ratio but in terms of optimum and maximum class size. The desired average seemed to be no more than 30 students in "practical" classes and no more than 60 in "theoretical" classes. No justification was suggested for the latter criterion.

In terms of teaching hours for individual professors, 2 universities had set a maximum of 15 hours per week and one a maximum of 24 hours per week. One rector reported that full-time professors were expected to teach at least 3 courses but no more than 4.

When asked how they saw their role in planning, the 42 responding directors suggested that they could provide the most assistance in helping to estimate quantitative and qualitative demand and supply in their professional area (9 responses), in collaborating with the university council on university-wide studies (8), in improving instruction and research within the faculty (7), in program-planning (7), in offering the university service (6), or in advising in the area of the faculty's special competence (5).

Clearly, for the most part, long-range planning and budgeting to match are just beginning to take place in the provincial universities. However, it is also clear that good ideas about future directions abound and that the time is ripe for coordinated efforts within and among the provincial universities to set long-range objectives and, above all, to discuss those objectives with the universities' constituents, intramural and extramural.

STUDENT AFFAIRS

The university's response to both social demand for admission and economic demand for graduates is inevitably reflected in its policies on admission and in its special services to students in their training and in their transition from the university to the professional world of work. Here, we look at some of the policies and practices of the provincial universities in the field of student affairs.

Admissions

Mexican universities, like those of most other countries, have had a series of crises arising from rapidly increasing social demand for admission. The pressure has been particularly acute in the Federal District. In 1964, UNAM announced the requirement of an additional year of *preparatoria* for entrance to the university. This had the effect of providing the university with one year of breathing space to take care of the huge backlog of unaccepted admissions requests from previous graduating *preparatoria* classes. After 1964, UNAM had to adopt a policy of restricted admissions for candidates from outside the Federal District. This policy increased the pressure for admission to the provincial universities, particularly those in close proximity to the Federal District.

This study does not purport to make a demographic analysis and projection of student population growth in the secundarias and preparatorias. Evidence of growth of the universities themselves over the time span 1961-67 is provided in Chapter 6. Here, we look at present policies for admissions, student services, and placement, as the deans and rectors report them.

Rectors and deans are consistent in reporting that entrance examinations are required of candidates for admission to most of the faculties of the provincial universities. Of the 66 deans, 56 indicated that admissions examinations were required of all students entering all professional carreras within their faculties. Two indicated that admissions examinations were used primarily for transfer students; 6 indicated that their faculties did not use admissions examinations; and 2 did not answer the question. In general, admission test requirements have been established rather recently with a median date of 1964 or 1965 for most universities and faculty types, although the examination requirements are some years older in faculties of medicine and in the universities of Guadalajara and Nuevo León.

Most admissions examinations (32 out of 43 described) are simple, non-standardized, short-answer tests oriented toward the material to be studied in the particular faculty. (Students enter the professional faculty of their choice directly from secondary school.) Generally, examinations are not standardized, and no reliability or validity studies were reported. Occasional use is made of multiple-choice aptitude tests or even personality tests. One dean reported using examinations of the College Entrance Examination Board. Apparently, examinations generally are scored by hand.[7]

At least one university has a university-wide policy of admission rather than a separate faculty-by-faculty procedure, and at least one university relies on its own preparatory school to do much of the screening. But by and large, each faculty of each university operates with a fair degree of independence in making and scoring tests, organizing admissions procedures, and making decisions.[8] It can be inferred that there are no cooperative arrangements among universities for constructing, standardizing, scoring, or analyzing the validity of test results or for regional or national administration of such tests.

Twenty-seven directors indicated that preparatory school record is taken into account in making the final decision on admission. Apparently, this record usually is considered in terms of a minimum average rather than in terms of some statistical weighting of grades or class rank with test results. Since many of the students come from the university's own preparatory school, this policy probably has more validity than it otherwise would. Eleven faculties require admissions interviews; 8 of these are included in the 27 that use secondary school records as well as examinations.

Geographical restrictions were reported by 20 of the 66 deans. The largest proportion of the 20 came from the universities of San Luis Potosí and Michoacán, whose policies necessarily are affected by the more restrictive policies of the institutions of the nearby Federal District. By the same token, heavy demand for entrance to schools of medicine and engineering has forced geographical restrictions in these fields.[9] Most directors see a continued tightening of admissions requirements in the future.[10]

Given the severe financial constraints noted elsewhere, it is not difficult to see why even the public state institutions are forced to think in terms of restrictive admissions policies rather than expanded services.

Promotion

Retention and drop-out rates of the several types of faculties are discussed at the end of this chapter. Of interest here are the directors' reports of policy regarding the promotion of students.

The majority of faculties require a student to pass all his subjects in order to be promoted, although a substantial minority indicate that passing all but two, or passing more than half, will satisfy promotion requirements.[11] Most stringent promotion requirements seem to be held by faculties of engineering, economics, and business administration. In general, there seems to be a policy of keeping students moving in their chosen carreras, as the evidence of "through-put" in Chapter 6 suggests. As indicated in Chapter 1, in comparison to other Latin American universities, Mexican universities have a relatively low drop-out rate.

Counseling

The comparatively low drop-out rate seems to be related more to increasingly selective admissions, or perhaps to an ethic of work and independence, than to organized systems of individual counseling or guidance.[12] The lack of a regular system of counseling through individual faculty-student relationships reflects in large part the fact that course programs are relatively fixed and there are few course options available. Once the student has chosen a particular faculty and has been admitted, all else follows automatically. If he decides to transfer to another faculty, he must begin the process all over again without transfer of credit. When these ground rules are understood, there is little need for professorial advice on alternative routes to a variety of educational and vocational goals.

Placement

That many of the faculties see little need to aid the student in his transition from classroom to professional practice is apparent in the responses regarding information on alternatives for employment made available to the student by the faculty or the university. According to the responses of directors, at only 3 of the universities (Veracruz, the Technological Institute of Monterrey, and Guadalajara) do as many as 2 faculties systematically attempt to provide employment information--not necessarily placement--to students, while only 2 of the universities (the Technological Institute of Monterrey and Sonora) appear to have an office (bolsa de trabajo) to service the entire university in this respect. Among the various types of faculties, only those of natural sciences (4) and economics and business administration (5) seem to consider this kind of service to be important.

Despite the relative lack of formal employment information services offered by the universities, the deans of faculties do have a rather clear idea of the best sources of information outside the university. The best sources seem to be private industry and the local chambers of commerce (18 responses) and "personal contact" (8 responses). The suggestion seems to be that students should make their approach directly to the company of their choice, although a few directors indicate that some industry-wide information on employment opportunities is sent to the university. In general, there is an implicit or explicit indication that it is more important to know someone than to have systematic information on types of opportunities. The best sources of information on employment outside the region seem to be federal agencies (7 responses)--from the Comisión de Fomento Minero to the Instituto Mexicano del Seguro Social to the Supremo Tribunal de Justicia--and private industry (7 responses). It is not clear, however, how the student himself is informed of even these general sources. The Mexican student makes his vocational decisions, like his educational decisions, very much on his own or with help from family and friends rather than from university officials. However, the university is much more helpful in providing students with information about programs of post-graduate study and post-graduate fellowships.[13]

It would be interesting to consider the informational aspect of the advising process from both the student's and the employer's point of view. One suspects that both parties would prefer a somewhat more efficient flow and display of information. The notion is sometimes advanced that the best arrangement for human resource development must involve a fairly precise assessment of future economic demand for various types of higher-level manpower and a matching of this demand by an equivalent supply of the required manpower through the educational system. The present writers tend to resist such a highly mechanistic formulation, particularly since, in fact, the trained professional often does shift fields and he, like the society he serves, is probably the richer for it. Yet, even given complete freedom of choice, choices do have to be made and informed choices usually are better than uninformed choices. As in all countries of the world, better economic information, particularly projections of manpower needs, undoubtedly could be profitably used by Mexican university students. Since there is little mobility among faculties and even among _carreras_ within faculties, it is probably important that such estimates of future demand be supplied to students early in their university careers. Even more important is the need to communicate to students the significance of new kinds of courses and course materials to the future practice of a given profession. The professional flexibility and mobility provided by the mastery of methodologies and techniques that are not limited to individual professional specialties should be made equally clear.

The efforts of the administration to improve the quality of the teaching faculty are less impressive than the efforts of the individual professor to improve himself. Administration seems to be more a program of survival--of making do with all too little--than an opportunity to experiment, to change, and to develop. The harsh financial constraints override all else. The administrators have good ideas, but there is little room for maneuver. The budgetary process is an annual doling out of funds rather than a vital tool for the planning of change, so new administrative services in support of students and student activities are unlikely to be instituted.

Efforts at university-wide planning are under way, but finished planning documents were not available at the time this study was made. Cooperative inter-university efforts in the field were mentioned by deans and have now come to fruition through the formation of the new National Planning Center for Higher Education. If the resources are lacking, vitality is not. With a demographic push from below, an economic pull from above, and a vital spark within, the provincial universities must and will change. It is equally clear that the change must and will be more than mere increases in size.

NOTES

1. In most universities, the final decision on the size of the faculty budget rests with the university council (27 primary responses--5 universities), the rector (18 responses--2 universities), or the trustees (5 responses--one university).

2. Ten directors indicated that the distribution of funds within faculties was ultimately decided by the rector and/or treasurer after consultation with the director; some (4) stated that the university council or trustees really had the final word; and some (3) replied that some sort of fixed quota was at work, with distribution of funds very much dependent on the distribution in the previous year.

3. Professors do play some part in the preparation of the budget in that they recommend promotions and new appointments (according to 15 deans); they submit lists of physical needs including equipment (12); the academic council of the faculty has the right to propose budgetary modifications (4); or professors are asked to report on their use of previous budgetary allocations (2).

4. Thirty-nine directors answered the question "What changes have occurred in the budgetary system

in the last five years?" Of them, 15 indicated that no changes had taken place; 12 simply said that budgets had increased as enrollments had increased; and 8 suggested that budgets had been used to effect changes in the appointment procedures, to change salary schedules, or to start new carreras. In addition, each of the following responses appeared once: change in the distribution of funds within faculty; a reduction in research funds; failure of funds for equipment and laboratories to keep pace with rising enrollments; and failure of funds for faculty appointments to keep pace with numbers of students.

5. To the question "Si no se han abierto nuevas fuentes de ingresos, cuales son los obstáculos que lo han imperido?" ["If new sources of revenue have not opened up, what are the factors that have prevented their appearing?"] the rector responded:

> Por falta de un serio estudio de planeación universitaria que permita conocer los fines que persigue la Universidad y los diferentes problemas que se le presentan para realizar una extensa campana para darla a conocer, para despertar interes por ella y para organizar una intensa actividad de promoción económica.
>
> [The lack of a serious study in university planning that might show the aims the university is seeking to realize and the various problems it faces and the lack of an extensive campaign to make itself known, to awaken interest in it and to organize an intensive effort at economic promotion.]

6. Sample response to the question "La Rectoría de la Universidad solicita información y colaboración de las Facultades y Escuelas, en los trabajos de planeación y desarrollo, y en que forma?" ["Does the president's office seek information and collaboration from the faculties in its work in planning and developing and in what form?"] is:

> Si. Solicita anualmente un informe completo de actividades de la Escuela o Depen-

dencia, asi como una enumeración de planes para el siguiente ciclo escolar, tanto planes de estudio como administrativos y de funcionamiento.

[Yes. It asks for a complete annual report of the activities of the school or other unit, as well as a listing of the plans for the following academic cycle--plans of study as well as administrative and operational plans.]

7. Directors indicate that sometimes a multiple-choice aptitude test is used for admission (6 responses), sometimes a more comprehensive achievement test is administered (2), and occasionally a personality test must be taken (3). The test usually is made up by a group of professors assigned to the task (29 of 44 responses), although occasionally it is prepared by the directive council of the school (3), under the direct supervision of the director of the school (4), or even under the supervision of the rector himself(3). Four directors indicated that professors of the university's preparatory school produced the examination, and one indicated that examinations were based on those of the College Entrance Examination Board. In general, they are corrected, apparently by hand, by the group that made them up, although 6 directors indicated that professors from the psychology departments were assigned the task and one noted specifically that examination results were electronically processed.

8. Of the 56 directors who responded to the question, 43 indicated that the decision on admission was made by some authority or committee within the faculty; 7, largely at one university, indicated that the decision was made, university-wide, under the auspices of the rector; and 6 indicated that the decision was made through the university's preparatory school or guidance department.

9. Fifteen directors reported that preference in admission was given to residents of their state, and 5 additional directors indicated a policy of

special preference for graduates of the university's own _preparatoria_. Nine of these 20 directors were at the universities of San Luis Potosí and Michoacán, and 10 of the 20 were deans of faculties of medicine or engineering.

10. Directors see a future tightening of admission procedure (9); the addition or improvement of tests (15); the addition of new secondary grade or course requirements (5); increased geographical restrictions (2); or the imminent introduction of admission tests for the first time (6).

11. Of the 62 responding directors, 36 said that students must pass all subjects to be promoted to the next university year; 11 indicated that the requirement was to pass half the courses; 11 others reported that students must pass all but 2 subjects; and 4 noted other special requirements. Promotion policies seemed consistent among faculties in 4 of the universities but not in the other 5. Most stringent promotion policies apparently are found in faculties of economics and business administration, with 8 of 11 faculties requiring passes in all subjects, and in engineering, with 10 of 16 faculties indicating the same policy. (For F test among faculties, $p = .291$--not significant; among universities, $p = .004$.)

12. Most of the university faculties (42) have some arrangement for educational and vocational guidance. However, this usually seems to be in the nature of group guidance organized under the _consejo técnico_ or the possibility of getting rulings on course and program requirements from the _junta académica_ of the faculty (15 instances). The next most common form of guidance is through informal chats with professors who are directors of individual courses or particular programs (14 responses). Sometimes, a series of seminars is organized (5 responses). Only 7 directors reported a system of assigned faculty advisers, and only 2 mentioned the availability of a professional psychologist for counseling. (No statistically significant differences appear among faculty types or universities.)

13. Of 66 directors, 54 indicated that information about post-graduate study and post-graduate fellowships is systematically provided to students. Information most often (24 responses) is provided through a central office of the university (e.g., Comisión de Becas; Departamento de Extensión, Departamento de Difusión Cultural; Departamento Escolar; Departamento de Orientación, la Rectoría, or la Secretaría de la Universidad). Alternatively (19 responses), a committee or office of the faculty takes on the job and acquires its information directly from other universities, foreign and domestic, and particularly from UNAM. Sometimes (7 responses), professors and directors of *carreras* collect the information somewhat informally, and sometimes (4 responses), groups of students get together to collect it.

CHAPTER 6

SOME STATISTICAL MEASURES OF GROWTH, RETENTION, AND FINANCIAL SUPPORT

A statistical appendix was attached to the questionnaire form submitted to the rectors of the nine universities. At least some appendix material was provided by all universities, and in certain instances it was possible to round out missing material from ANUIES sources. Data were requested at the level of the individual faculty in order to obtain comparisons both among universities and among types of faculties. The brief summary of these data that follows is presented both to establish norms or base lines for future comparisons and to introduce the reader to some of the variables that will be subjected to multivariate analysis in Appendix A.

SIZE AND GROWTH

Appendix Tables 47 through 49 provide a summary of the size of faculties as of 1967 and their growth after 1961. Of note in both the size and growth figures is that most of the distributions, particularly distributions within faculty types, are rather sharply skewed, with means considerably larger than medians. (Distributions within individual universities are more normal.) The median (or middle) figures are better descriptions of the "typical" faculty because the mean values are considerably affected by a relatively few very large "atypical" faculties.

Typically, the largest faculties are those of law and economics, followed by medicine and engineering, with faculties of agriculture, natural science, and philosophy the smallest. Median registrations range from 571 in law to 174 in philosophy, with corresponding mean enrollments of 719 and 201. The largest faculty in 1967 had an enrollment of 1,766, while the smallest had a total of 48 students. In 1961, the comparable extremes were 1,336 and 13. Mean enrollments systematically exceed median enrollments in all types of faculties. The most notable difference occurs among medical schools: The typical (median) faculty is of size 280, but a few very large faculties raised the overall average size (mean) to 559.

In Chapter 1, the general growth of Mexican higher education in years 1961-67 was indicated. Total enrollments at the professional level in Mexico grew from about 77,000 in 1961 to about 150,000 in 1967. In the nine universities under study, the growth during the same period represented a comparable doubling--from 18,000 to 38,000. However, the percentage growth was considerably more rapid in the smaller faculties, as indicated by the mean percentage gain of 160 per faculty reported in Appendix Table 48. Although it may appear that this high percentage gain per faculty gives a somewhat distorted picture of overall gain (precisely because of the relatively large number of small faculties), it is nevertheless an important index since it suggests the considerable reorganization that must have been necessary in the small faculties. The tripling of the size of a small faculty from 100 to 300 students (200 percent gain) represents a much smaller absolute gain than an increase from 1,000 to 1,500 students in a well-established large faculty, but it probably requires more dramatic change in program, instruction, and other services to students than the growth of the larger faculty.

It is clear from Appendix Table 48 that the most dramatic rates of growth have been taking place in the faculties of economics and business administration (presumably in the smaller ones) and in the faculties of philosophy, natural science, and agriculture (most of which tended to be relatively small in 1961).

The growth statistics are displayed in different form in Appendix Table 49, where the mean position of each type of faculty is reported in terms of standard deviations above or below the mean of all faculties in 1961 and 1967. For those faculties for which data were available in both 1961 and 1967, a comparison was made of the relative standing in those two years and the relative gain or loss is reported in the third column. Again, it is clear that greatest relative gains were made by faculties of economics and business administration, followed by those of agronomy and philosophy. Engineering faculties, which on the average were second only to law faculties in size in 1961, suffered a loss in size relative to other types of faculties (although they had a median gain of 28 percent as indicated in Appendix Table 48). In terms of faculty size, engineering faculties now follow faculties of medicine and economics as well as law.

Interesting changes in standing occurred among universities. The universities in the city of Monterrey (the Technological Institute of Monterrey and Nuevo León), which had responded earlier to the enormous growth rate of that urban area (see Chapter 1), although still among the four largest universities in absolute terms, had given way in terms of _rate_ of growth to the other seven universities, particularly those of Guadalajara and Veracruz (with branches in both Jalapa and Veracruz). These seven universities are now feeling the kind of expansion in higher education already experienced by both the Federal District and the city of Monterrey. The smaller universities (Guanajuato, Michoacán, San Luis Potosí, and Sonora) also made striking percentage gains and gains in relative standing. In contrast, the growth of the faculties of the Universidad del Estado de México has been less spectacular.

It seems clear that the new wave of social demand for admission is being experienced (and accommodated) in the smaller more peripheral universities, particularly in the development-related and less costly faculties of economics and business administration. Faculties of engineering, which earlier experienced an extremely high rate of growth, are now lagging at least in relative terms, no doubt because of the relatively high cost of education in such faculties and because of a conscious policy of greater selectivity in admissions. A compensating growth in subprofessional programs (carreras cortas) in engineering specialties apparently is only beginning to take place, although such programs would serve to provide alternatives to professional training and thus increase overall retention.

It is clear that insofar as social demand in the provinces is being satisfied, it is being satisfied primarily by the provincial universities since admission to institutions in the Federal District is now considerably restricted. Although data on the geographic origin of students were not available in 3 of the universities studied, it is clear that over 80 percent of students in the other universities (with the exception of the large, private Technological Institute of Monterrey) come from the same state in which the university is located (see Appendix Table 55). This is particularly true of faculties of law and medicine, which are generally older and have served local demand for a longer time. Students are more apt to cross state lines to obtain degrees in the new disciplines of agronomy and the natural sciences.

With 34 reporting faculties, the mean percentage of students from within state is 75 percent, 21 percent from other Mexican states, 2 percent from the Federal District, and 2 percent from foreign countries.

RETENTION

Retention figures are surprisingly high in the universities under study (see Appendix Table 50). The percentages reported are the ratio of last-year enrollments in 1966 and 1967 to first-year enrollments in 1961 and 1962, for those carreras that are five years in length. For six-year medical carreras, only 1967 and 1961 figures were used in establishing the ratios. This gross estimate of retention ignores migrations into the faculty, drop-outs who return, "repeaters," and those who drop out in the final year. Nevertheless, it is a more accurate estimate of retention than the more usual comparison of first- and last-year enrollments in any given calendar year. The median figure of 50 percent, although undoubtedly an over-estimate of actual retention in a cohort group, is certainly higher than comparable measures in most other countries of Latin America and probably higher than comparable figures for public undergraduate institutions in the United States. There still is room for improvement in retention rates in the average faculty of philosophy or natural science and in some of the faculties of each of the other types, but the real room for improvement would seem to lie in the quality of instruction and research more than in efficiency as measured by "through-put" of students. As will become apparent in the multivariate analysis in Appendix A, retention is not easily predictable from independent measures of quality or instructional capacity. For example, average retention appears to be best in schools of law, which fall behind most other types of faculties on the majority of the other variables measured.

Although the data collected for this study do not permit an estimation of retention prior to the 1961-67 period, it is of interest that the percentage gain of final-year enrollments from 1961 to 1967 greatly exceeds the percentage gain of first-year enrollments during the same period. Of the 43 faculties for which first-year enrollments were reported from 1961 to 1967, there was a mean gain of 43 percent and a median gain of 38 percent. For the 39 faculties for which final-year enrollment figures were available, there was a mean gain of 317 percent and a median gain of 177 percent. Of course, it should be noted that both the first-year and the last-year figures (particularly the latter) are much smaller and less stable than total enrollment figures. Further, the largest percentage gains undoubtedly occur in the smallest and least stable faculties (statistically speaking). Nevertheless, the difference in gains between first- and last-year enrollments is striking and clearly suggests that the present very high rates of retention are a relatively recent phenomenon.

FULL-TIME APPOINTMENTS

Systematic differences do occur both among types of faculty and among universities with reference to another important variable: the percentage of professors who hold full-time appointments (see Appendix Table 51). Professors of agriculture and natural science, one-third and one-quarter of whom are, respectively, full-time appointees, lead the list, while professors in the older faculties of medicine and law have the smallest proportion of full-time appointments, with 5 percent and 6 percent, respectively. The Technological Institute of Monterrey, Sonora, Neuvo León, and Veracruz have the highest proportion of full-time faculty members among universities with respective percentages of 43, 30, 26, and 21, while at each of the other five universities in the study, fewer than 10 percent of the professors serve on a full-time basis.

The study attempted to discover the proportions of full-time faculty in the years 1963 and 1965 as well as in 1967, but, although data for 69 faculties in 1967 were received, only 31 faculties were able to report figures for 1963 and 37 faculties for 1965. For what the figures are worth comparatively, the proportion of professors with full-time appointments was 18 percent in 1963 and 1965 and 16 percent in 1967. Again, the same faculties are not being compared, but the data are at least suggestive. With rapid expansion in the demand for admission, universities must obtain more professors. Even if the university has provision for an increased number of full-time appointments, it means little if the salaries and long-term career opportunities are not competitive. The university, then, has to continue to fall back on the hourly professor who supports himself in other ways but who, as we have seen, is apparently willing to devote an increasing proportion of his time to university affairs.

EXPENDITURES

Although the proportion of professors who hold full-time appointments seems to be related positively to a number of other measures of instructional capacity or quality (see Appendix A), the proportion of university budgets spent on professors' salaries is related negatively. This apparent paradox is, of course, explained by the positive relationship between measures of quality and expenditures on items other than direct instruction--particularly administration, research, library, and student services. Appendix Table 52 reports the differences for this variable among faculties and among universities. Most notable is the relatively low proportion of the budget that is spent on professors' salaries in faculties of agronomy and medicine and at the Technological Institute of Monterrey. Despite the theoretically heavy non-instructional costs in natural science and engineering faculties, the proportion of budget going for salaries exceeds 70 percent; expenditures on laboratory and library equipment and services are proportionately small.

The overall average expenditure per student in the science-related faculties suggests very inadequate expenditures on faculty salaries as well as other kinds of services (see Appendix Table 54). Although the mean expenditure per faculty in the natural sciences approaches adequacy at $600 per student per year, the median figure of $290 indicates that it is only in a minority of the science faculties that expenditures even exceed the very low overall average of $314 per student per year in the universities in our sample. (See Chapter 1 for international comparisons.) Admittedly, the figure is unrefined and results from a raw division of total budgets by total enrollments with no attempt to estimate full-time equivalents for students. Nevertheless, by any standards the amount is exceedingly low and the figure for law schools falls short even of that expended for primary school students in many countries. Among the universities, expenditures per student per year exceeded $1,000 only at the Technological Institute of Monterrey, with those in Sonora a distant second at $372.

Although an attempt was made to get exact figures for expenditures on laboratories and libraries, it was possible to get such budgetary information only from a small minority of faculties. Of the 18 faculty budgets listing specific library expenditures, 10 indicated expenditures of approximately 1 percent of the total faculty budget and only 2 faculties listed expenditures of more than 3 percent of the total faculty budget. Median laboratory expenditures for the 17 reporting faculties were 6 percent of the total faculty budget, with 4 listing expenditures of over 10 percent of the total faculty budget. (Absolute values of library expenditures are discussed in Chapter 4 and reported in Appendix Tables 42 and 43.) Again, by any standards these expenditures are low both in absolute terms and relative to other expenditures.

USE OF CLASSROOMS

Available data on use of classrooms are summarized in Appendix Table 53. However, such data are not used in the multivariate analysis (see Appendix A) because they were available for the majority of faculties in only 3 universities. Even fewer faculties reported on weekly use of laboratories. The average number of hours of use per classroom per week was 29 (24 faculties reporting); the comparable figure for laboratories was 25 (23 faculties reporting). In general, classrooms and laboratories are used most efficiently by medical schools, a fact that is no doubt related to the clinical nature of instruction with relatively more hours in class per course.

Quantitative measures of absolute and relative growth, retention, and expenditures are of obvious interest to planners in and of themselves. However, our real purpose was to explain them in anticipation of their use as criterion variables in several different types of multivariate analyses, which are to be found in Appendix A.

CHAPTER

7

CONCLUSION

A general discussion of the sample used for this study is presented in Chapter 2. In a certain sense, the sample permits the application of the results of an analysis of nine universities to the whole system of higher education in Mexico, or at least to a great part of it, since the system is largely composed of institutions that are public in character.[1]

What picture of the Mexican university does the study give us? The following summary is intended to recapture the most important elements of the completed research from which we will attempt to draw some conclusions that may serve as possible avenues for immediate action and as points of reference to other studies that are already being reported.

SUMMARY OF DATA

General Points

1. The Mexican universities are growing and changing more in response to social demand for education than as a result of coordinated planning.

The author of this chapter is Lic. Alfonso Rangel Guerra, Secretary General of Mexico's National Association of Universities and Institutes of Higher Education

2. According to present university laws, the aims of the university are to conserve, transmit, enrich, and increase the society's culture. In some cases, the university laws include aims related to the function of the university in Mexico's society, particularly in terms of regional interests.

3. In comparative international terms, the $300 expenditure per pupil per year on higher education in Mexico is low. Comparable dollar figures reported by the OECD in 1964 included the following: Asia as a whole, $400; Latin America as a whole, $600; and Africa as a whole, $1,000.[2]

4. Approximately half of the faculties and schools of the universities included in the sample were founded after 1950. A national study would indicate that the majority of faculties and post-secondary schools in the entire country also were founded after that year.

5. Since high-level human resources are a necessity for regional development and universities are a source of such resources, development of the regional universities must be regarded as a matter of national interest.

Teaching Faculty, Instruction, Plans, and Programs

1. In most cases, changes in programs of study are simply the addition or rearrangement of courses without an attempt to reorient the student's approach to learning.

2. New faculties and schools or new-degree programs have course curricula as rigidly fixed as those already in existence, with few options and few possibilities for transfer of credit from one faculty or one program to another.

3. The reorganization of programs often consists of adding a new <u>carrera</u>, new courses, or another academic year; shifting subject matter from one year to another; joining two <u>carreras</u> into one; or

combining courses--all administrative changes that do not substantially alter the nature of the studies themselves.

4. When they do occur, the most important changes in the content and methodology of programs are introduced by professors with advanced training.

5. The great majority of university professors are young. Half of those who responded to the questionnaires completed their professional training in 1959 or later and therefore were approximately 30 years old at the time of the survey in 1968.

6. Approximately 20 percent of the part-time professors and 60 percent of the full-time and half-time professors have undertaken post-graduate study. These percentages are important, particularly in the case of part-time professors. But it must be noted that incentives for graduate study, including the promise of professional advancement upon receipt of the master's or doctor's degree, do not exist for either full-time or part-time professors. In any case, the increasing numbers of professors who do graduate work on their own are beginning to change the traditional image of the professor who simply hangs on without improving himself and thereby contributes to the immobilization of the university.

Research

Very little research is carried on in the Mexican provincial universities. According to the replies of 55 of 66 deans of faculties and schools, the teaching faculty does not receive incentives for research.

Libraries

Of 66 deans of faculties and schools, 58 affirmed the existence of a faculty library. However, only one dean indicated holdings of more than 10,000 volumes, while 70 percent reported holdings of less than 2,700 volumes. The mean annual budget for acquisitions for faculty libraries is $1,300. The typical faculty library has only one full-time employee, usually a high school graduate without university training or training in library science who receives a monthly salary of about $100. Figures from another study show that, of 220 university librarians surveyed, only 4 held a library degree, only 9 held a university degree of any sort, and only 53 had pursued studies beyond high school.[3]

Administration and Budgets

1. The two most important factors in the process of budgeting seem to be the demand for admission to the university and a comparison with the budget of the previous year. Apparently, changes in educational aims, programs, and procedure are not considered in establishing the budget.

2. Budgeting is considered more an administrative necessity than a process of communication and a potential mechanism for ordering priorities among middle- and long-range programs.

3. Many of the deans' responses express the need for administrative and program change and indicate a recognition of the important role that the budgetary process can play. However, none of the deans' responses clearly specify the policies, procedures, and techniques that might provide a fundamental change in the process.

4. The ability of an institution to realize its aims depends in large part on the support that the administration gives to the program.

5. As emphasized in the statistical analyses in Chapter 6 and Appendix A, there are wide qualitative differences among the instructional capabilities of Mexican universities. These differences are positively related to expenditure per student and negatively related to rate of growth of enrollments. Thus, growth and development are not synonomous, but both require investment.

The preceding points attempt to define and summarize in general terms the conditions of higher education in Mexico. Some proposed courses of action for the solution of problems of higher education follow.

ANALYSIS

Determination and Justification of the Objectives of Higher Education

It is necessary to review the traditional assumptions about the nature and aims of higher education that are built into current university law, to identify the aims that are in accord with current national realities, and to indicate conditions that will make the realization of national aims possible. This work has already begun and forms part of the Preliminary Analysis of Higher Education, a study carried out by the National Planning Center for Higher Education and published early in 1970.[4] In the study, the following statement is made:

> The recent development of the nation, both by its nature and its speed, has served to highlight with increasing intensity the role which education must play in the processes of social and economic change, as it responds dynamically to social and economic demands.
>
> Those who are trying to respond to these demands by diminishing the obvious present disjunction between education and the needs of society underline the urgent need to define in clear operational terms the way in which the educational system must organize itself so as to stimulate the processes of change and development. In other words, what is needed today, as always, is a clarification of educational objectives, the very definition of which will help the system to move in a rationally chosen way.[5]

Educational Planning at the National and Institutional Level

At the time the survey for this study was carried out, almost no one was working in educational planning at the level of higher education. Today, with the establishment of the National Planning Center for Higher Education under the auspices of the National Association of Universities and Institutes of Higher Education and with the creation of departments or offices of planning in more than ten universities, work is under way to study and define institutional problems and future directions. But it is necessary to sharpen and to elaborate procedures in order to capitalize on and expand work already done.

The growth of institutions of higher education must be regulated and directed through planning, for only in this way will it be possible to establish solid bases for institutional development and transformation. The training of professionals in planning is essential.

Social demand for admission to higher education must be satisfied, but not in a haphazard way; rather, the demand must be satisfied in terms of regional and national needs, and educational service must change in response to those needs. The necessary allocations of resources for programs at the institutional, regional, and national level can better be made by persons with training in planning.

To some degree, the pressure and accumulation of problems and the lack of funds in institutions of higher education prevent planning and related activities directed toward the future. Nevertheless, work done at both the national and institutional level since 1968 indicates that the vicious circle has been broken and that the complex situation is being attacked through efforts to identify and understand the current problems of higher education.

Training of Professors

If an educational institution has a high-quality, full-time faculty whose members are professionally up-to-date and informed about new ideas in teaching and research, then the institution is capable of the continuous change, renewal, and adaptation that its development demands. The moving force in the classroom, in the laboratory, and in the entire university community is the professor. By the same token, it is the professor who is responsible for the successes and failures of the educational effort and on him, in the last analysis, rests the image that the whole institution acquires--an image that can either reflect change and transformation or rigidity of structure, content, and aims.

The fact that a good percentage of university professors undertake graduate studies at the master's and doctor's degree levels at their own expense is positive, but it is not sufficient to assure the quality and quantity of higher educational services that the country needs. Educational institutions must be promotional agents in expanding and improving their own teaching staffs. The urgent and immediate need of the contemporary Mexican university is to undertake the preparation of its own professors, not only to face the problem of improving and bringing up-to-date those who are already teaching but also to enlarge faculties in order to satisfy the growing demand for higher education.

The university should be capable of training and preparing its own faculty members, just as it trains and prepares professionals and specialists for industry and other professions that are fundamental to national interests. And the professionals will emerge from the university better trained and prepared if the university itself has more and better-trained professors. Professors are important in the life of the university, and a program to train and prepare them would have favorable repercussions in all aspects of university life from the moment the graduates of new programs began to teach. The universities should be concerned not only with the training of faculty members but also with conditions that will affect them: e.g., salaries, offices, laboratories, laboratory equipment, libraries, and library services--whatever assists the new professor to capitalize on his training and become part of the renovation and change of the institution itself. A high-quality teaching faculty knows how to exert its influence to renew teaching methods, plans, programs of study, academic organization, and the very life of the institution.

Expansion of Research

Expansion of research activities is closely related to the training of professors and to the entire reform of higher education. Increased research depends in large part on the members of the teaching faculty, their plans and programs of study, their instructional methodology, and their ability to foster in the individual student an interest and concern in exercising his highest rational and intellectual abilities.

Economic resources are essential for research but do not in themselves guarantee research activity; lack of research is not entirely due to lack of funds. Again, as in other areas of education, resources should be applied to concrete specific programs leading to the transformation, renovation, and change of traditional structures.

In August 1970, a study was completed by the National Institute of Scientific Research at the request of the Secretariat of the Presidency, carried out in collaboration with a number of institutions throughout Mexico.[6] The study analyzes the current status of scientific and technological research and recommends specific programs for the development of research. It is interesting that, in a chapter describing instruction and research, the picture of higher education in Mexico coincides largely with that described in this study.

Importance of Libraries

The importance of truly effective library services to any basic reform of higher education cannot be overemphasized. The training of librarians is urgently needed so they can establish procedures and techniques to support the central university libraries and the libraries of faculties and schools. Adequate libraries are essential to any program of instruction both inside and outside the classroom.

According to this study, the lack of library resources and services is the most critical aspect of higher education in Mexico, and this lack affects all aspects of instruction. It is not possible to conceive of a library with adequate holdings, organization, and services as an adjunct to a stationary, traditional, and routine system of instruction; nor is the reverse situation possible. Libraries and teaching, with all that they imply, must be developed and renewed simultaneously.

Administrative Organization

Two fundamental aspects of administrative organization must be considered: structure and personnel. The data gathered for this study show that the need for change in the structure of administrative organization is beginning to be considered. It is important to note that the nascent concern for developing an administration that not only serves academic activities and research but also facilitates the process of change is in part a result of the very forces for change that are currently being forced upon the universities themselves. The change in administrative personnel is closely related to the change in structure. It became obvious some years ago that the appointment of full-time professors could no longer be postponed since higher education could not continue to sustain itself exclusively with part-time professors. Now it is necessary to realize that Mexican universities cannot get along with administrators who dedicate only a minimal part of their time to administrative affairs as a distraction from their professional activities. What is needed now is the professional full-time administrator who can effect fundamental change in the institution's internal and external systems of communication. Just as the university needs planners, professors, and librarians who are specially trained for their professional roles and tasks, so it needs administrators who are not mere improvisers but understand fully their area of action and its vital importance to the total life of the institution.

Administration is more than technique: It is understanding. It is toward a better understanding of the many factors of institutional growth and development and their inter-relationships that this study has been directed.

NOTES

1. See Chapter 2. In 1967, the 9 universities considered in the sample represented 54.3 percent of the student population at the level of higher education in the 68 public institutions of higher education outside the Federal District. The 78 faculties and schools included in the study represent one-third of all faculties of public institutions outside the Federal District.

2. Financing of Education for Economic Growth (Paris: OECD, 1966).

3. Carl M. White, Mexico's Library and Information Services: A Study of Present Conditions and Needs (Totowa, N.J.: Bedminster, 1969).

4. National Planning Center for Higher Education, Diagnóstico Preliminar de la Educación Superior (México: ANUIES, 1970).

5. Ibid. See particularly the following sections by Olac Fuentes Molinar: "Sobre los objetivos del sistema de educación superior en México," "Objetivos educativos y realidad del sistema de educación: Un análisis de disfuncionalidades," and "Objetivos educativos y realidad de las instituciones de educación superior: Las condiciones de su ajuste."

6. See Política Nacional y Programas en Ciencia y Tecnología (México: Instituto Nacional de la Investigación Científica, 1970), Part II, Chapters 2, 3.

STATISTICAL APPENDIXES

APPENDIX

A

A MULTIVARIATE ANALYSIS

In the previous chapters, an attempt has been made to describe in summary form numerous characteristics of professors and characteristics of schools as reported by their directors. The descriptive variables have been compared among faculty types, among universities, and between hourly and non-hourly professors when such comparisons have seemed worth highlighting. However, the variables have not been compared or correlated with each other. It is to this effort that this appendix is directed.

Many of the descriptive data reported in Chapters 4 and 5 are categorical rather than continuous and are not amenable to correlational analysis. That is to say, they are often tallies of different kinds of responses to the same open-ended question, with not one of these responses considered "better" or "larger" than the next. (For example, similar directors' responses to the question on recent changes in the practice of their respective professions have been grouped together--categorized--but no attempt has been made to rank-order the groups in terms of the "importance" or "significance" of the response.) However, a number of variables do measure amount (e.g., _number_ of books in the library, _number_ of articles written) or are ratings of the quality of response to a particular item or series of items that may themselves be categorized rather than continuous. It *is* possible to correlate these variables with each other and it *is* possible, by subjecting them to such multivariate techniques as factor analysis, regression analysis, and discriminant analysis, to better understand certain underlying dimensions with which the study is concerned. The availability of standard computer programs makes the application of these techniques to punched-card data relatively easy. Factor analyses and regression analyses reported below were performed using DATATEXT routines on an IBM 7094. Discriminant analyses were performed using programs developed by Kenneth Jones based on the analysis described in William W. Cooley and Paul R. Lohnes.[1]

FACTOR ANALYSIS OF PROFESSORS' RESPONSES

Since literally dozens of the variables describing professors and their activities are continuous in nature and since there are almost that many continuous variables describing directors' opinions, policies, and procedures, it is useful to reduce the very large matrixes of inter-correlations to more manageable dimensions. Factor analysis provides one such method of data reduction as it permits us to consider a limited number of dimensions (factors) each composed of variables that hang together. At the same time, it makes possible a more comprehensive and cohesive interpretation of the characteristics of professors and of schools, at least as defined by the responses to the questionnaire used in this study. The so-called principal-component factor analysis employed here further locates the dimensions in such a way that each is orthogonal to (or uncorrelated with) the previous one; thus, each is a genuinely "new" dimension in explaining differences among professors or directors and can be measured by its variance in relation to the total variance of the whole body of data.

Appendix Table 56 reports the principal-component factor loadings for the first 6 factors of an analysis of 69 professors' variables. The reported standardized weights show the relative importance of the contribution of each variable to the factor.

The variables most heavily weighted in the positive direction on the first factor include variables 1, 19, 21 to 30, and 32. These describe a non-science professor (variable 1) who is apt to be a graduate of a university in his own state (19), is relatively young (21), is apt to have gone to a private institution (22) or to the university in which he is now teaching (23) or to one of the "special" Mexican universities--i.e., UNAM or the Technological Institute of Monterrey--(24), has graduated relatively recently (26), and is apt to have gone on to post-graduate study in another institution in the same state as the one in which he is now teaching (27) or to the actual university in which he is now teaching (28) or to one of the "special" Mexican universities--i.e., UNAM or the Technological Institute of Monterrey--(29), from which he is apt to have graduated relatively recently (32). Large negative weights are associated with number of laboratory hours per week (5), number of publications produced (36 to 38), professional societies joined (39), average and total laboratory hours per week (46 and 47), average number of students (48), average and total number of assistants (50 and 51), and use of non-Spanish-language journal articles in instruction (64 and 65). This first factor can be said to describe the locally well-trained non-science professor.

It is clear that not all of the positive weights are necessarily desirable (variable 1--science and non-science--is neither desirable nor undesirable) and not all of the variables with negative weights are undesirable (variables 36 to 38 related to scholarly production are supposedly desirable rather than undesirable). The weights simply define a dimension that explains, to a large degree, differences among professors. For example, universities necessarily employ both scientists and non-scientists. On the factor just described, scientists will tend to get negative scores and non-scientists positive scores. On the other hand, variables associated with graduate study are probably *ipso facto* good and will tend to give less negative scores to those scientists who have done graduate study. Productive research, however, slightly increases the negative direction of the score in this particular dimension. The reverse happens on factor 6, which is a research factor. Professors at the Technological Institute of Monterrey and Nuevo León are the only ones who average a positive score on factor 1, presumably because the positive weights for the post-graduate variables outweigh the negative weights for the research variable.

Factor 2 seems to define the full-time teacher (variable 2) who has office hours for students (6), makes good use of a central library (11 to 15), attended school outside the state in which he is now teaching (17 to 19), responds interestingly to the open-ended questions on changes in his profession (41 to 43), has a relatively small class (44) and number of students per week (48), and makes relatively heavy use of non-Spanish texts (54 and 55), non-Spanish reference books (60 and 61), and non-Spanish journals (64 and 65). This factor does seem to be more of a quality factor describing the well-educated, "modern," full-time career professor. In this instance, the most positive average factor scores emerge at the Technological Institute of Monterrey and the University of Sonora.

Factor 3 seems to describe the locally trained scientist who devotes most of his energy to laboratory instruction. Most positive scores appear at Nuevo León and San Luis Potosí.

Factor 4 has to do with sheer weight of teaching load, while factor 5 has to do with more traditional forms of instruction involving relatively heavy use of *apuntes* and essays and reading materials primarily in Spanish. Factor 6, as previously noted, appears to be a productivity or research factor.

The factor solution is both reassuring and suggestive. It is reassuring in that the factors seem to make sense. Variables that one might expect *a priori* to cluster together do seem to do so. This suggests, in turn, that the individual variables are measuring what they are supposed to measure. It is suggestive insofar as some factors or some portions of factors do seem to hang together as measures of quality, modernity, or instructional capacity. The normative information reported in the previous chapters takes on added significance precisely for these measures that seem to fit with each other. If dimensions of science or non-science research and instruction can be identified empirically through statistical data reduction, these may well be worth considering as targets for institutional or associational action.

FACTOR ANALYSIS OF DIRECTORS' RESPONSES

A factor analysis also was made for 67 of the variables resulting from the responses of directors. This analysis is reported in Appendix Table 57. Factor one is particularly strong as it accounts for 15 percent of the variance of the entire system of measures and contains more than twice the variance of any other factor. This factor has to do with the presence or absence of cooperative programs among faculties (variables 6 to 9), the substance and quality of responses having to do with changes in the practice of the respective professions and the schools' responses to such changes in their own programs and in community-service programs (variables 10 to 15, 25, and 26), research and incentives for professors to do research and to participate in programs of self-development (variables 19, 20, 23, 30, 32, 33, and 54), and use of central library services (variables 35 to 37 and 49). In short, it is a factor having to do with cooperative internal services and response to external needs. The weights are consistently negative rather than positive because the responses are skewed to the lower end of the scale being used to measure them. In a sense, the factor is upside down or reversed. Directors responding most frequently with positive responses to the above clusters of variables are to be found at the Technological Institute of Monterrey and the universities of Guanajuato and Veracruz.

Factor 2 is somewhat more difficult to describe but has to do primarily with the size and services of faculty libraries (variables 38 to 48). This cluster of variables, in turn, is related (weights are in the same direction) to science as opposed to non-science faculties (variable 1) and faculties in which research is related to instruction (variable 16). Directors responding most positively on these variables are to be found at the universities of Sonora, Nuevo León, and Veracruz.

Factor 3 is related to the recent establishment of programs of research and programs for the recruitment and development of teaching faculty. (Note that the weightings for variables 21 and 29 are strongly positive while the weightings for the items dealing with the various aspects of the research and faculty-development programs are negative. This factor is also upside down.) The directors whose faculties seem to have been most active recently in initiating such programs are to be found at the universities of Guadalajara, Veracruz, and Guanajuato.

The other factors are less significant and harder to define and they begin to duplicate some of the elements of earlier factors.

It is a truism that a factor analysis can only show what was put into it in the first place. That is to say that a factor analysis is completely dependent on the choice of variables to be analyzed. Admittedly, a substantial portion of the questions asked of the directors had to do with their opinions of changes in their professions and their schools' reactions to such changes. Nevertheless, factor one is of particular interest not only because of its strength but because it does show that directors' responses on matters of professional change and program change do hang together. These, in turn, seem to have a good deal to do with development of teaching faculty and with elements of support for instruction, particularly central library services. The inter-relationship of faculty development and library development with other positive characteristics of schools and professions emerges throughout this study and is merely highlighted once again in the factor analysis.

REGRESSION ANALYSES OF PROFESSORS' RESPONSES

Regression analysis seeks to combine mathematically a set of "independent" or "predictor" variables in such a way as to maximize their joint or multiple correlation with some meaningful criterion or "dependent" variable. Put another way, it is an attempt to see how much of the variation of a dependent variable can be explained (predicted) by a set of independent variables acting together.

It was decided to investigate the relationship of both professors' and directors' variables to the following criterion measures: the rate of retention of students, the relative rate of growth of enrollments, a qualitative ranking of universities, and a qualitative ranking of types of faculties. The first two criterion variables are described in Chapter 6. Retention is important as a measure of efficiency of the educational system in producing graduates, while the relative rates of growth of faculties are indicative of their respective responses of social demand for admission. The last two variables result from a subjective ranking of universities and faculties within universities made according to an overall judgment of quality by members of the ANUIES staff. Since the rankings are subjective, the regression analyses, in a sense, serve only to indicate what kinds of considerations probably seem most relevant to members of the ANUIES staff in their thinking about measures of quality in member institutions. Nevertheless, the relative importance of predictor variables should be instructive.

Appendix Table 58 lists the uncombined or "zero-order" correlations of the four criterion measures with the professors' variables that appear to be the most interesting on the basis of the factor analysis just described, on the basis of an examination of the full correlation matrix of all continuous variables, and on the basis of an examination of the numbers of professors responding to each term. Beside each column of zero-order correlations are a few figures in parentheses. These are the so-called Beta weights, which indicate the relative importance of those variables that in combination produce the highest correlation with the criterion. At the bottom of the column of Beta weights are the respective multiple correlations (multiple R's) and the R^2s, which are a more exact measure of the proportion of variation in the criterion variable that is predicted, or explained, by the predictor variables. The analysis of the retention-criterion variable excludes the Technological Institute of Monterrey, since criterion data for the years 1961 to 1963 were lacking for that institution.

The correlations with the subjective rating of quality of the universities made by the ANUIES staff are more consistent in sign than are those with the other criteria. In general, variables having to do with positive aspects of training or teaching are related positively to the criterion, while hourly load and student load are related negatively. This is to be expected since the questionnaires were designed by officials of ANUIES in the first place. The few variables that combine to give the best prediction of institutional ranking are whether a professor attended UNAM or the Technological Institute of Monterrey or a university other than his own in the same state, the number of hours per week he is available to students for consultation, and whether he uses the central library to put books on reserve for his classes. Variables combining with negative weights are the use of _apuntes_ (professors who make heavy use of fixed lecture notes tend to be in universities with lower ratings), total hours of class per professor per week, and whether the professor attended his home university. This last variable has a low zero-order correlation with the criterion and is a so-called "suppressor variable" that takes on a high weight opposite to the one with which it is highly related--in this case variable 22. (The positive aspect of variable 22 has to do with that part of the variable not measured by variable 21.)

With the exception of the special statistical relationship just noted, both the zero-order correlations and Beta weights do seem to make sense. The universities judged to be better seem to have a larger number of professors who: have outside training; are full-time professors; hold office hours for students; make good use of a central library, books, and other publications in other languages as well as in Spanish; have original ideas about changes in their professions; make corresponding changes in their courses; and do not have heavy class loads even though they tend to be full-time rather than hourly professors. Although the basic purpose in collecting data on these topics was to establish normative levels rather than to predict a subjective ranking of universities, the fact that the predictive relationship makes sense does serve to validate the normative data.

The prediction of the ranking of faculty types emphasizes a different set of variables primarily because the science-related faculties tend to be ranked higher than the non-science faculties. Thus, variables having to do with laboratory instruction (such as total laboratory hours per week and number of assistants) take on positive weights. The weights for central library use shifts because certain faculty types (medical schools, for example) tend to use their own faculty libraries rather than a central library, even though the latter is available for use.

The rate of growth of an individual faculty as compared to the average rate of growth of all faculties is less predictable from the professors' variables than are the criteria of instructional capacity or quality. We know from our table of institutional means (Appendix Table 49) that faculties of economics have much the highest rate of relative increase while faculties of engineering are losing ground in relative terms. Thus, it is not surprising to find variable 1 (faculty type) appearing as one of the major variables in the regression equation or to find variable 42 (laboratory assistants) appearing with a negative weight. By the same token, the relative loss of ground by the Technological Institute of

Monterrey and the University of Nuevo León serves in large part to explain the negative weights for variables 14 (use of central library reserve shelves) and 22 (graduation from UNAM or the Technological Institute of Monterrey). The positive weight for variable 40 (average number of students per course) reflects the relatively rapid growth, for example, of the University of Guadalajara, which is the university with the largest average class size (see Appendix Table 28).

The regression analysis of retention should be examined in light of the mean retention figures reported in Appendix Table 50. Since law schools, which have very large classes and heavy teaching loads (see Appendix Tables 26 and 28), have a surprisingly high reported rate of retention and since schools of natural science and philosophy have, relatively, much smaller average class size, lower teaching loads, and lower rates of retention, it is not surprising to discover a positive relationship between class size (variable 41), teaching load (variable 42), and retention. In fact, retention seems to be unrelated or negatively related to variables that seem to measure qualitative aspects of instructional capacity except perhaps for variable 22 (graduation from UNAM or the Technological Institute of Monterrey).

REGRESSION ANALYSES OF DIRECTORS' RESPONSES

The low or negative correlations of retention with measures of instructional capacity are even more striking for the directors' variables (see Appendix Table 59). The great majority of variables related to such positive policies as institutional support for research, for inter-faculty cooperation on instruction, for use of central library and improvement of faculty library, and for recruitment of professors are negatively related to the criterion of retention. Although the rate of retention per faculty is surprisingly well predicted, the prediction results from negative correlations with "good" variables or positive correlations with such variables as variable 53 (number of course failures allowed in promotion of students) or variable 58 (dean attended graduate school at his own rather than at an "outside" university). Variable 30 having to do with the central library is a good variable with a positive weight, but it should be noted again that this is not affected by the Technological Institute of Monterrey since that university has been excluded from the retention analysis for lack of criterion data in 1961 and 1962.

In short, retention in these faculties is not positively related with positive characteristics of professors or with positive faculty policies reported by the directors. It is the custom of educational planners or educational economists to focus on rates of through-put and to point out the relationship of those rates with cost per graduate. It is not our intention to depreciate that exercise but rather to point out that a high rate of retention, although a good index of efficiency, is no guarantee that worthwhile things are happening to the student while he is being put--or even hurried--through. Admittedly, this study does not attempt to measure direct educational outputs through achievement tests administered to students. Nevertheless, its indirect measure of quality based on questionnaire responses has a certain amount of face validity. In any case, the variables are surprisingly consistent in direction (signs) in statistical terms.

It is greatly to the credit of all faculties--good, bad, and indifferent--to have reached the high average level of retention indicated by Appendix Table 50 and corroborated by more recent unpublished studies of the new National Planning Center for Higher Education. Yet, a high level of retention or through-put, even in areas that seem to match economic demand for graduates, is not in itself proof that the educational system is operating effectively or efficiently except in terms of that limited criterion alone. Good retention is a necessary but not a sufficient element of effectiveness. It is the intent of this study to suggest a series of measures that, at least at face value, have some relevance both to the quality of education and to its effectiveness in regional development.

The institutional characteristics described by directors that seem to be the best predictors of relative rate of growth (see Appendix Table 59) are the following: older institutions (variable 2) with larger numbers of subprofessional carreras (variable 3) whose directors are concerned with external changes in the profession (variable 10) but which are doing relatively little to improve their teaching faculty (variables 27 and 28) or to improve their faculty library holdings and services (variable 42). The multiple correlation with the criterion of relative gain in enrollments is a surprisingly high .80. The predictive variables suggest that there are some faculties distinguished less by quality of teaching and research than by social responsiveness. If the pressures for admission are great enough, they must be accommodated somewhere. Clearly, a number of the faculties at the provincial universities must so respond and, in the absence of independent junior colleges, must begin to offer subprofessional-level work within the university. Apparently, this is beginning to happen.

The prediction of the subjective rankings of faculty types derived from subjective ratings of the quality of individual faculties within the nine universities essentially is related to an underlying dimension of science versus non-science. In general, the ratings of science-related faculties are higher. For this reason, we have purposely omitted variable 1 (our code for faculty type) because by itself it correlates .80 with faculty rankings. Of the remaining variables, the best predictor of faculty-type quality is, somewhat ironically, a negative weighting of the number of books in the faculty library. This is explained by the fact that the non-science faculties of philosophy, economics, and particularly law tend to have larger numbers of volumes in their faculty libraries than do the science-related faculties (see Appendix Table 40). It is perhaps even more ironic that law schools, which have the largest present holdings, have the least adequate budgets for current acquisitions (see Appendix Table 42). Since the law schools are the oldest of the faculties, the relative size of their holdings is not surprising, but the small size of the annual budget for current acquisitions casts some doubt on the quality or modernity of these holdings.

The other negative Beta weights in the regression equation that best predict the rankings of faculty types are not quite as easily interpreted. Faculties rated higher appear to have deans who did not do graduate work at their present institutions and who tended not to cite many changes in their professions. This latter variable (number 9) appears in the equation primarily because of its pattern of inter-correlation with other predictor variables rather than because of a high zero-order correlation with the criterion. (The direct correlation with the criterion is only —.07.) Yet, there is some logic to it in that the deans of medical schools, which rank high, mentioned few changes in the profession (see Appendix Table 39), while deans of economics faculties, which ranked lower, noted many. This fact also suggests that faculties were not ranked according to their responsiveness to changes in their respective professions.

Factors rated positively with rank of faculty type include incentives to professors to do research (variable 22) and incentives to professors for self-development and promotion (variable 28). These factors apparently are more characteristic of science-related faculties.

As with the professors' variables, the great majority of the "good" directors' variables are either positively related to the rating of quality of the university or essentially unrelated. Few have negative weightings. The multiple correlation of the best few of these variables with the criterion (.60) is not as striking as might be expected from an examination of the zero-order correlations by themselves because of the relatively high inter-correlation among the best predictors.[2]

The variable related to number of volumes in the faculty libraries now takes on a positive weight because we are comparing universities (the average of all types of faculties within individual universities) rather than types of faculties. Other variables entering positively in the regression equation are the quality of the deans' responses to the question on changes of the profession (variable 10), the quality of response on community courses (variable 24), and positive responses to the questions on incentives provided to professors for professional self-development (variable 28). Other variables with relatively substantial positive weights include positive opinions on inter-faculty cooperation (variable 7), incentives to professors to do research (variable 22), and placement and advisory services to students (variables 55 and 56). Taken together, all these variables suggest that the ratings of quality are in some way related to the attention shown by the university to individual professors and students.

REGRESSION ANALYSES OF ACTIVITIES INDEXES

It is only fair to point out that variables having to do with the quality of a dean's response have as much or more to do with the dean's persuasiveness as with the objective facts of that faculty's policies and procedures. We have tried to shed some further light on the inter-relationships of directors' opinions, policies, and practices by creating 5 activity indexes that roughly correspond to certain major descriptive topics in the previous chapters. The first of these is an index of inter-faculty cooperation made up by a simple combination of variable 5 (number of cooperating faculties), variable 6 (number of types of cooperative instructional arrangements among faculties), variable 7 (a sum of the positive opinions of directors regarding inter-faculty cooperation), and variable 8 (a rating of the quality of the director's response to all the questions on inter-faculty cooperation in instruction).

Appendix Table 60 reports the regression analyses. Inter-faculty cooperation is best predicted by the number of extra-university cooperative arrangements (variable 14), appointments of non-full-time assistants in the faculty library (variable 40), the number of changes that have been made in the central library (variable 43), and the existence of a service that provides students with information about post-graduate programs (variable 56). Predictors with negative weights include variable 60 (the number of courses the dean teaches) and variable 61 (the percentage of overall retention).

These results suggest, of course, that internal and external cooperative arrangements tend to go together--in this case, the criterion of faculty cooperation on instruction, external cooperative arrangements for research (variable 14), and the cooperative effort that is necessarily implied by the development and improvement of a central library (variable 43). These arrangements take some administrative guidance, so it is apparently no coincidence that inter-faculty cooperation is negatively related to the number of courses the dean teaches. Once again, retention seems to correlate negatively with a set of worthwhile internal activities. Emphatically, this is not to say that high retention is bad. On the contrary, it is merely to say once again that it is an important but limited measure (of quantity) and not necessarily a good index of quality.

The multiple correlation of the above six predictors with the criterion was a very respectable .74. Variables that have positive correlations with the criterion but did not enter the regression equation because of relatively high inter-correlations with the other predictor variables were incentives to professors to do research (variable 22) and recruitment of professors (variable 47). Of passing interest is the negative correlation of the criterion of inter-faculty cooperation with relative gain in enrollment. Here again, a good quantitative measure correlates negatively with a qualitative measure.

The second activities index analyzed was "program changes," a simple combination of variable 11 (whether or not there have been recent program changes in the faculty), variable 12 (the number of such changes), and variable 13 (the rating of the quality of the directors' responses to the open-ended questions on program changes). Faculties that have tended to institute changes are large (variable 2), older schools (variable 1) that recently have added one or more new <u>carreras</u> (variable 3) and are concerned with faculty recruitment (variable 25) and changes in budgetary procedures (variable 45). Program changes are positively related to central library changes and negatively related to faculty library changes. This result tends to describe faculties of economics and, secondarily, faculties of natural sciences; among universities, it describes the Technological Institute of Monterrey, Veracruz, and Guanajuato.

The multiple correlation with the index of program changes was .65, which is substantial but not spectacular. Of course, change in and of itself is not necessarily good. Yet, as an index it does indicate some degree of responsiveness to external changes and perhaps even suggests the possibility that new programs are a cause of external change.

Our third internal index was for research activities. This category included variable 16 (number of reported researches), variables 17 and 18 (the quality of the directors' responses to a general open-ended question on research and to one on the relation of research to instruction), and variable 19 (whether the faculty was engaged in research in cooperation with outside institutions). Most of the positive qualitative responses by deans correlated positively with this criterion, while the quantitative criteria of retention, size, and growth correlated negatively. The variables that emerged in the best regression equation had to do with faculty recruitment, advising of students, and the faculty's role in university planning. Apparently, faculties engaged in research are particularly concerned with the individual professor and the individual student, even if their rate of retention of students is less than that of faculties not engaged in research.

An index of the number of community courses offered by the individual faculties and the quality of the dean's response in describing such programs was best predicted (multiple R of .73) by the number of subprofessional programs offered by the faculty, whether the faculty offers incentives to professors to do research, and whether the faculty advises students regarding possibilities for post-graduate study and fellowship support. Negatively weighted variables were the dean's teaching load and the number of faculty library assistants (note positive correlation with the central library item, variable 43). The positively weighted items suggest an institutional social concern that transcends the mere production of more graduates for professional practice as of old.

Finally, an analysis has been made of an index of staff development made up of responses and ratings of responses to questions on programs of faculty improvement and economic incentives to professors to engage in professional self-development. Positive predictors include incentives to research (variable 22), available bibliographic services (variable 37), and extent of faculty recruitment (variable 47). From the negative weights for variables 1 and 67, we infer that highest degree of faculty development is taking place in older faculties that are not growing as rapidly as the average.

Appendix Table 61 reports the inter-correlations of the above indexes with each other and with an index of central library services that was not analyzed separately because it is something of an artifact of the relatively extensive use of the central library in only 3 universities. All correlations are positive and all but the research index (variable 91) produce a majority of inter-correlations that are statistically significant at the .05 probability level (one asterisk in the table) or at the .01 level (two asterisks). Of special note are the high inter-correlations among inter-faculty cooperation, community service, and staff development. The approaches to social response and qualitative improvement differ widely among individual faculties and even among types of faculties and among universities. Yet, it is of interest that indexes of activities in these three rather disparate areas are positively related. In fact, this was indicated earlier in the chapter by our factor analyses. Elements of responsiveness, change, development, and modernization do seem to hang together, and perhaps in and of themselves they are worth reordering as a criterion of quality in relation to the nation's and ANUIES' aims for regional development. Furthermore, the correlations suggest that a faculty tends to develop or change in several ways at once.

DISCRIMINANT ANALYSIS OF PROFESSORS' RESPONSES

One final approach to multivariate analysis of our data is made here in an attempt to define those dimensions of professors' characteristics that seem to best distinguish universities from each other. We already have distinguished universities from each other according to the mean factor scores deriving from the factor analysis described at the beginning of this chapter. But the mathematical criteria for establishing the weights for each factor emphasized the cohesiveness of certain elements in the factor rather than their ability to distinguish one group (university) from another. Here, we shall apply a mathematical method that weights the variables in such a way as to produce a dimension (factor) that maximizes the variance among groups relative to the variance within groups.[3] That is to say, it assigns weights in such a way that the means of the groups (in this case, the universities) will be as far apart from each other as possible. It will then be of interest to see which variables take on the largest weights because these will be the variables that best explain the differences that exist among universities. It should be emphasized that the method is not designed to rank universities but simply to highlight their differences.

Appendix Table 62 presents the scaled, or standardized, weights for the 22 variables on the first 4 discriminants. The weights are standardized in the sense that they may be compared in size directly with each other even though the variables with which they are associated have very different scales. We present vectors for 4 discriminants only because the fifth and succeeding discriminants do not provide discrimination among groups significantly better than chance. In discriminant analysis, the first discriminant in effect locates the axis or hyperplane that most effectively separates the groups being studied. The successive discriminants attempt to maximize group differences in terms of the variance that remains after that of the first discriminant has been removed. Consequently, the first discriminant always accounts for the largest proportion of variance among groups. Hence, it is always the most significant discriminant. In this instance, the probability that the separation provided by the first discriminant could have occurred by chance is .1804E-20 (a decimal point followed by 20 zeros and a 1804). The first three discriminants are very highly significant.

The professors' variables that best distinguish universities from each other (first discriminant) are: the proportion of full-time appointments (variable 2); the professors' use of central library reserve shelves (variable 6); their fluency in a foreign language, usually English (variable 11); and teaching load (a relatively low number of total hours of class per week on variable 15 and a relatively low number of students per class on variable 17). Other variables of note on the first discriminant are number of hours of student advising (variable 4) and use of non-Spanish texts (variable 20). Use of _apuntes_ (variable 5) and graduation from the local _preparatoria_ (variable 9) have negative weights. The positive weight for variable 1 (faculty type) indicates that universities that have a relatively high proportion of non-science faculties will receive a positive score on this discriminant. The first discriminant could be described as a modern-traditional dimension, with those institutions whose professors receive large negative scores representing the characteristics and practices of the more traditional professional university with its more separated faculties, part-time professors, and heavy student load. It is of interest that the ranking of institutions in this first discriminant (see Appendix Table 63) is closely correlated with the expenditures per student reported in Appendix Table 54.

With the removal of the major dimension described above, the succeeding dimensions become somewhat more difficult to interpret. The professors who received positive scores in the second discriminant tend to be in non-science fields (variable 1), to be hourly professors (variable 2), to require essays of their students (variable 7), to have attended _secundaria_ and _preparatoria_ away from the states in which they are now teaching but to have attended their present universities (variables 8, 9, and 10), to have good ideas about changes in their professions, and to teach large classes and a large total number of students (variables 13, 17, and 18). This dimension apparently gives high scores to the faculties that are bearing the heaviest brunt of the massive demand for admission (compare with faculty size in Appendix Table 47). Not surprisingly, the University of Guadalajara scores highest on this dimension (see Appendix Table 63).

No attempt is made to interpret the third and fourth discriminants except to remind the reader that they are only significant by themselves when one keeps in mind the variance that has been removed in the first two discriminants.

By applying the appropriate weights to the original variables for each professor by computer, one obtains a discriminant score for each professor. By then averaging the discriminant scores for all professors within each university, it is possible to obtain the so-called centroids (means) for each group, which are reported in Appendix Table 63. Of course, it should be recalled that we are making this analysis on the basis of a sample of professors from each of these institutions and that, despite cautions to the contrary, the sample in any given institution may not be completely representative.

It is clear that the data from the Technological Institute of Monterrey tend to dominate the first discriminant. That is to say, to a considerable extent they determine its positive extreme. That the data and the combination of discriminants are valid for the entire system despite the influence of the Technological Institute of Monterrey can perhaps be suggested in another way. The computer program used for the analysis permits not only the computation of discriminant scores for each professor but also the computation of a combination of his discrimination scores, which can then be compared with the mean or centroid score of each university. It is thus possible to indicate the distance of each professor from each group centroid; to put it another way, it is possible to classify professors according to the university to which they are most likely to belong. Appendix Table 64 reports such a classification of the professors in our study. If the weights resulting from our discriminant analysis are applied to each of the coded responses of the 53 professors from the Technological Institute of Monterrey in our sample, 39 receive centour scores that are closest to the centroid of the Technological Institute of Monterrey while 7 are closer to (look more like) the professors at Nuevo León, one is closer to San Luis Potosí, and so forth (follow the figures in <u>row</u> 6 of Appendix Table 64). Thirty-nine of the 53 would thus have been correctly classified as professors at the Technological Institute of Monterrey if we had had only the answers to their questionnaires and no information about their actual group membership. Column 6 reports the number of professors from other universities who would have been incorrectly classified as teaching at the Technological Institute of Monterrey: These include 5 professors actually at Veracruz and 3 at Nuevo León.

Of our sample of 327 professors, 142 are correctly classified ("direct hits"). If classification had been done at random among the 9 groups, the expected number of direct hits would have been 36. Of course, the purpose of this exercise is not really to classify professors but rather to suggest that there are institutional differences with respect to characteristics of professors. The number of misclassifications in any given column is a measure of the extent to which the professors at that institution are like those at other institutions. Column 4 (Nuevo León) and column 9 (Veracruz) show that a relatively large number of professors at other institutions would be misclassified as teaching at Nuevo León or Veracruz if our analysis were done "blind." This suggests that Nuevo León and Veracruz are the most prototypical of the 9 universities under study. Conversely, the most unique would be Sonora (column 8), the Technological Institute of Monterrey (column 6), Michoacán (column 4), and Guadalajara (column 2).

The computer program for the discriminant analysis provides a summary that indicates how close the group centroids are to each other. Appendix Table 65 is a reconstruction of that summary ordered in such a way that the universities whose professional characteristics are most alike appear closest to each other. The off-diagonal figures in each _row_ indicate how far from the given institution's centroid the other institutional centroids fall. The figures in the _row_ for the Technological Institute of Monterrey indicate that the centroids for Sonora, Nuevo León, and Veracruz fall at points closer to the Monterrey centroid than do 3 percent of the actual professors at Monterrey. The _column_ for the Technological Institute of Monterrey indicates that the group centroid for Monterrey falls closer to the Sonora centroid than do 4 percent of the professors at Sonora, closer to the San Luis Potosí centroid than do 1 percent of the professors at San Luis Potosí, and so forth.

The size of the off-diagonals in each _row_ is a measure of the heterogeneity of the professors' characteristics in a particular institution. Thus, the characteristics of professors at Sonora are much more heterogeneous than those at the Technological Institute of Monterrey. The size of the off-diagonals in each _column_ is a measure of how unique or prototypical the institution in question is. Thus, the characteristics of the professors at Sonora are more diverse than are those of the professors at Nuevo León (as indicated by the respective row distributions), but the average at Sonora is less prototypical than that at Neuvo León (as indicated by the respective column distributions).

The Appendix Table 64 as a whole suggests that it is possible to distinguish these 9 universities from one other in quite dramatic fashion in terms of the measure of characteristics of the sample of professors from each institution. Caution should be exercised in interpreting the weights of the several discriminants, particularly since the method is designed merely to emphasize differences among groups and not to measure or to rank-order the quality of the groups with respect to one other. Nevertheless, it is clear that some of the groups differ from each other rather strikingly. For example, combined professorial characteristics show more significant institutional differences than do rates of retention or growth. (The first discriminant is statistically much more significant than the differences among means for retention and growth.) All of which suggests that what is most important about institutions may not be merely their size and output but a number of internal characteristics as well. Obviously, an institution of small size and minimal output will have little social significance. By the same token, however, large institutions with high output may be emphasizing quantity rather than quality; if support is inadequate, they may be doing so out of sheer necessity.

Clearly, both quantity and quality are important, particularly at a time of rapid demographic growth. The universities are under tremendous pressure to respond to social demand for admission. The temptation is to respond in the least expensive way and to measure success in terms of quantitative output alone. That there is a grave risk in this approach is suggested by the fact that the qualitative differences that do in fact exist among faculties and universities become irrelevant if quantitative output is the only criterion. The measures of quality or instructional capacity reported here are not positively related to retention. Retention and quality are essentially independent dimensions in the Mexican universities. Both must be taken into account in planning future growth; both are important; and both cost money; but both are related to regional development; and the variables of instructional capacity, at least, are related to institutional change. If the effect of the university on regional development involves more than mere increase in numbers of graduating professionals--and it seems obvious that it must--then factors of instructional capacity and social response must receive the investment they deserve.

NOTES

1. Kenneth Jones, _The Multivariate Statistical Analyzer_, multilithed (Cambridge, Mass.: Harvard University Press, 1964); William W. Cooley and Paul R. Lohnes, _Multivariate Procedures for the Behavioral Sciences_ (New York: John Wiley, 1962).

2. The addition of a predictor variable that is relatively highly correlated to those already in the equation adds less predictive power to the equation than does the addition of a variable that is essentially uncorrelated with the other predictors.

3. For a discussion of the mathematics and computational routines for the discriminant function, see particularly: T. W. Anderson, _An Introduction to Multivariate Statistical Analysis_ (New York: John Wiley, 1958), Chapter 6; J. G. Bryan, "The Generalized Discriminant Function," _Harvard Educational Review_, Vol. XXI, No. 2 (1951), 90-95; Cooley and Lohnes, _op. cit_., Chapter 4; Jones, _op. cit_.; C. R. Rao, _Advanced Statistical Methods in Biometric Research_ (New York: John Wiley, 1952), Chapter 8.

APPENDIX B
DESCRIPTIVE TABLES

Appendix Table 1

Median Date of Founding of Professional Faculties of Universities Operating in 1967

Faculty	All Mexico	Nine Universities in Sample
Law	1854	1870
Medical and dental sciences	1943	1952
Architecture and engineering	1949	1953
Agronomy and veterinary medicine	1962	1953
Economics and business administration	1957	1949
Philosophy, humanities, and other	1959	1959
Natural sciences	1957	1954

Source: La Tecnología de la Enseñanza en las Universidades Mexicanas--Datos Básicos (México: ANUIES, 1968).

Appendix Table 2

Student Enrollments at the Nine Universities in Sample in Comparison to Rest of Mexico

University	Post-grad-uate	Profes-sional	Egre-sados*	Secon-dary	Total
Guanajuato	--	1,980	(283)	2,366	4,346
Guadalajara	4	9,284	(1,053)	8,972	18,256
Estado de México	--	1,473	(144)	2,249	3,722
Michoacán	--	3,311	(266)	3,967	7,278
Nuevo León	46	7,285	(939)	5,149	12,480
Monterrey	332	4,294	(416)	3,852	8,478
San Luis Potosí	--	2,492	(276)	3,805	5,297
Sonora	--	1,566	(94)	3,268	4,834
Veracruz	--	6,317	(517)	20,867	27,184
Total for nine universities in sample	382	38,012	3,988	53,475	91,875
Total for all state universities	446	69,781	(6,766)	107,924	178,151
Total for all universities in Federal District	2,452	81,035	(8,677)	95,287	178,774
Total (all associated universities)	2,898	150,816	(15,443)	203,211	356,925

*Egresados are essentially those students who have completed course work for a professional degree but have not yet completed a thesis and actually obtained the degree. The number of titulados--degree recipients--each year runs a bit more than half the number of egresados.

Source: La Educación Superior en México, 1967 (México: ANUIES, 1969).

Appendix Table 3

Financial Support of Mexican Universities, 1959 and 1967 (in millions of pesos)

University	Financial Support			
	Federal	State	Private or Special	Total
1967				
Guanajuato	5.8	7.0	.3	13.1
Guadalajara	14.5	15.3	4.2	34.0
Estado de México	4.9	6.7	.4	12.0
Michoacán	6.9	5.5	.4	12.8
Nuevo León	12.7	21.8	8.2	42.7
Monterrey	3.3	0	44.8	48.1
San Luis Potosí	5.6	2.0	1.5	9.1
Sonora	5.5	.4	26.0	31.9
Total (nine universities)	59.2	58.7	85.8	203.7
Total (all states)	137.6	138.1	113.6	389.3
Total (Federal District)	717.2	0	40.2	757.4
Total (all associated universities)	854.8	138.1	153.8	1,146.7
1959				
Total (all states)	19.8	58.1	8.4	86.3
Total (Federal District)	198.7	0	17.7	216.4
Total (all associated universities	218.5	58.1	26.1	302.7

Sources: La Educación Superior en México, 1967 (México: ANUIES, 1969); La Educación Superior en México, 1966 (México: ANUIES, 1967).

Appendix Table 4

Classification of Types of Faculties or Schools in Sample

Faculty Type	Total Number	Number of Directors Reporting
Medical and dental sciences	14	11
Natural sciences	12	10
Architecture and engineering	20	16
Agronomy and veterinary medicine	9	4
Economics and business administration	15	11
Law and social sciences	8	7
Philosophy, humanities, and other	9	7
Total	87	66

Appendix Table 5

Distribution of Directors in Sample by Type of Faculty
(number in parentheses indicates questionnaires returned)

University	Medical and Dental Sciences	Natural Sciences	Archi- tecture and Engi- neering	Veter- inary Medicine and Agronomy	Business Adminis- tration and Eco- nomics	Law and Social Sciences	Philos- ophy and Others	Total
Guanajuato	1(1)	1(1)	5(3)	0	2(0)	1(1)	1(0)	11(6)
Guadalajara	2(2)	1(1)	2(2)	2(2)	2(2)	1(1)	1(1)	11(11)
Estado de México	2(2)	0	2(2)	0	1(1)	1(1)	2(2)	8(8)
Michoacán	2(0)	0	2(2)	2(0)	1(1)	1(1)	0	8(4)
Nuevo León	2(2)	3(2)	3(2)	1(0)	2(0)	1(1)	1(1)	13(8)
Monterrey	0	1(1)	2(1)	1(1)	2(2)	0	1(0)	7(5)
San Luis Potosí	3(2)	2(2)	1(1)	1(0)	2(2)	1(1)	0	10(8)
Sonora	0	1(1)	1(1)	1(1)	1(1)	1(1)	1(1)	6(6)
Veracruz	2(2)	3(3)	2(2)	1(0)	2(2)	1(0)	2(2)	13(11)
Total	14(11)	12(11)	20(16)	9(4)	15(11)	8(7)	9(7)	87(67)

Appendix Table 6

Number of Professors' Questionnaires Sought and Obtained, by University

University	Full-time Professors			Non-full-time Professors		
	Sought	Obtained	Non-hourly*	Sought	Obtained	Hourly*
Guanajuato	9	9	12	28	20	17
Guadalajara	28	16	16	54	24	24
Estado de México	5	5	7	17	17	15
Michoacán	6	10	11	21	14	13
Nuevo León	36	28	29	53	36	35
Monterrey	39	36	36	22	16	17
San Luis Potosí	8	9	15	27	27	21
Sonora	12	7	7	10	6	6
Veracruz	25	24	31	22	22	15
Total	168	144	164	254	182	163

*Non-hourly figures include half-time appointees. Hourly figures do not include half-time appointees (see Chapter 2).

Appendix Table 7

Number of Professors' Questionnaires Sought and Obtained, by Type of Faculty

Faculty	Full-time Professors			Non-full-time Professors		
	Sought	Obtained	Non-hourly*	Sought	Obtained	Hourly*
Medical and dental sciences	27	22	30	68	34	26
Natural sciences	27	25	25	24	18	18
Architecture and engineering	44	35	36	44	38	37
Agronomy and veterinary medicine	20	13	16	17	12	9
Business administration and economics	32	29	33	50	42	38
Law and social sciences	6	7	9	30	24	22
Philosophy and humanities	12	13	15	18	15	13
Total	168	144	164	251	183	163

*Non-hourly figures include half-time appointees. Hourly figures do not include half-time appointees.

Appendix Table 8

Professors' Dates of Graduation from Preparatory School and University

Percentage of Professors Reporting Graduation Dates as Indicated	Preparatory School	University	
		First Professional Degree	Post-graduate Degree
90	1960 or before	1966 or before	1968 or before
70	1957 or before	1963 or before	1966 or before
50	1953 or before	1959 or before	1964 or before
30	1947 or before	1953 or before	1961 or before
10	1939 or before	1944 or before	1951 or before

Note: 242 of the 327 professors in the sample reported their dates of graduation from preparatory school; 292 of the 321 professors with professional degrees reported the dates the degrees were received; and 102 of the 131 professors with post-graduate degrees reported the dates the degrees were received.

Appendix Table 9

Median Graduation Dates of Professors

Faculty Type	Preparatory School		First Professional Degree		Post-graduate Degree	
	Mean Graduation Date	Number of Professors in Sample	Mean Graduation Date	Number of Professors in Sample	Mean Graduation Date	Number of Professors in Sample
Medical and dental sciences	1946	56	1954	55	1960	24
Natural sciences	1953	43	1959	42	1962	18
Architecture and engineering	1957	73	1962	70	1965	35
Agronomy and veterinary medicine	1956	25	1961	24	1966	11
Economics and business administration	1955	71	1960	69	1966	25
Law and social sciences	1945	31	1954	30	1967	6
Philosophy, humanities, and other	1954	28	1959	23	1962	10
F test for mean differences among faculty types	$p = .001$		$p = .001$		$p = .08$	
F test for mean differences among universities	$p = .179$		$p = .002$*		$p = .14$	

*Significance largely explained by average age of professors at University of Guadalajara (7 years above mean) and Guanajuato (4 years above mean).

Appendix Table 10

Location of Secundaria Attended by Professors

Present University Affiliation	Percentage Distribution				Number of Professors in Sample
	State of Present Residence	Federal Dis-trict	Other Mexico	Foreign Country	
Guanajuato	64	8	20	8	29
Guadalajara	85	0	15	0	40
Estado de México	65	23	12	0	22
Michoacán	83	9	8	0	24
Nuevo León	86	5	9	0	64
Monterrey	53	18	17	12	53
San Luis Potosí	77	6	17	0	36
Sonora	77	0	8	15	13
Veracruz	66	14	15	5	46
Total	--	--	--	--	327
Percent of total	64	8	25	3	--

Note: F test for differences among universities: $p = .006$.
F test for differences among faculty types in professors attending secundaria in present state of residence: $p = .05$. Highest percentages are for law and medicine, lowest for agronomy and philosophy.

Appendix Table 11

Location of *Preparatoria* Attended by Professors

Present University Affiliation	Percentage Distribution: Present State of Residence	Federal District	Other Mexico	Foreign Country	Number of Professors in Sample
Guanajuato	67	8	17	8	29
Guadalajara	79	7	11	3	40
Estado de México	55	36	4	5	22
Michoacán	75	21	0	4	24
Nuevo León	89	6	5	0	64
Monterrey	57	19	10	14	53
San Luis Potosí	81	8	11	0	36
Sonora	62	15	8	15	13
Veracruz	63	26	6	5	46
Total	--	--	--	--	327
Percent of total	69	16	8	6	--

Faculty Type	Percentage of Professors Who Attended *Preparatoria* in Present State of Residence	Number of Professors in Sample
Medicine	74	56
Natural sciences	68	43
Engineering	70	73
Agronomy	52	25
Economics	73	71
Law	90	31
Philosophy	44	28
Total	--	327

Note: F test among universities: $p = .08$.
F test among faculty types: $p = .01$.

Appendix Table 12

Location of Universities Attended by Professors

Present University Affiliation	Percentage Distribution				Number of Professors in Sample
	Present State of Residence	Federal District	Other Mexico	Foreign Country	
Guanajuato	65	15	16	4	29
Guadalajara	78	18	4	0	40
Estado de México	27	68	0	5	22
Michoacán	67	29	4	0	24
Nuevo León	89	9	2	0	64
Monterrey	68	15	3	14	53
San Luis Potosí	78	19	3	0	35
Sonora	31	31	23	15	13
Veracruz	50	39	6	5	46
Total	--	--	--	--	327
Percent of total	63	27	7	5	--

Note: F test among universities: $p = .000$.
F test among faculty types: $p = .11$ (not significant). On basis of faculty type, the major divergence from mean of 66 percent attending university in present state of residence is agronomy at 40 percent.

Appendix Table 13

Location of First Professional Training of Professors

Faculty Type	Percentage Distribution					Number of Professors in Sample
	Federal District	State of Nuevo León	State of Jalisco (Guadalajara)	Other Mexican States	Foreign Country	
Medical and dental sciences	30	11	35	24	--	56
Natural sciences	26	42	14	16	2	43
Architecture and engineering	19	37	10	28	6	73
Agronomy and veterinary medicine	32	44	--	20	4	25
Economics and business administration	21	30	24	22	3	71
Law and social sciences	16	16	45	20	3	31
Philosophy, humanities, and other	22	33	10	20	15	28
Total number	75	96	67	71	13	327

Note: F test for differences among faculty types in percentage of professors receiving first degree from university in present state yields $p = .11$.

Appendix Table 14

Number of Years of University Study Completed by Professors

Faculty Type	Percentage Distribution				Number of Professors in Sample
	4 Years or Less	5 Years	6 Years	More than 6 Years	
Medical and dental sciences	9	23	57	11	56
Natural sciences	42	46	7	5	43
Architecture and engineering	25	63	6	6	73
Agronomy and veterinary medicine	36	40	8	16	25
Economics and business administration	21	62	10	7	71
Law and social sciences	14	75	--	11	31
Philosophy, humanities, and other	23	54	19	4	28
Total	--	--	--	--	327
Percent of total	24	53	15	8	--

Note: F test among faculty types: $p = .000$. See Appendix Table 17 for differences among universities.

Appendix Table 15

Number of Professors Holding Post-graduate Degrees

Faculty Type	Percentage Distribution						Total Number with Some Post-graduate Study (percent)	Number of Professors in Sample
	Second Undergraduate Degree	Working Toward Masters	Masters	Certificate of Higher Specialty	Post-masters	Doctorate		
Medical and dental sciences	9	0	0	31	0	0	31	56
Natural sciences	7	5	14	7	0	9	30	43
Architecture and engineering	8	5	19	10	0	5	34	73
Agronomy and veterinary medicine	4	4	16	12	0	12	40	25
Economics and business administration	8	0	13	6	1	3	23	71
Law and social sciences	6	3	3	0	3	0	6	31
Philosophy, humanities, and other	7	7	7	0	0	11	18	28
Total	--	--	--	--	--	--	--	327
Percent of total	6	4	11	11	1	5	38	--

Note: F test yields $p = .72$ (not significant).

Appendix Table 16

Source of Graduate Training for Professors

Faculty Type	Percentage Distribution: Federal District	Nuevo León	Other Mexico	United States	Other Foreign	Number of Professors Reporting
Medical and dental sciences	38	0	0	54	0	24
Natural sciences	11	21	5	42	21	19
Architecture and engineering	17	37	6	26	14	35
Agronomy and veterinary medicine	8	23	0	62	7	13
Economics and business administration	20	32	12	28	8	25
Law	67	33	0	0	0	6
Philosophy	20	20	10	0	50	10
Total	--	--	--	--	--	132
Percent of total	22	24	5	34	15	--

Note: F test for differences among faculty types in percentage of professors doing graduate work in present state of residence: p = .04.

Appendix Table 17

Number of Years of University Study of Professors

Present University Affiliation	Percentage Distribution: 4 Years or Less	5 Years	6 Years	More than 6 Years	Number of Professors Reporting
Guanajuato	32	52	12	4	25
Guadalajara	13	53	16	18	38
Estado de México	23	45	18	14	22
Michoacán	39	31	26	4	23
Nuevo León	18	55	21	6	63
Monterrey	21	61	8	10	52
San Luis Potosí	25	56	16	3	32
Sonora	15	39	31	15	13
Veracruz	31	51	14	2	43
Total	--	--	--	--	311
Percent of total	24	52	16	8	--

Note: F test for differences among universities: p = .19.

Appendix Table 18

Level of Post-graduate Study Among Professors

Present University Affiliation	Percentage Holding			Number of Professors in Sample
	Higher Specialty (Certificate)	Masters	Doctorate	
Guanajuato	10	0	10	29
Guadalajara	5	8	3	40
Estado de México	5	9	0	22
Michoacán	25	0	0	24
Nuevo León	11	11	2	64
Monterrey	9	41	19	53
San Luis Potosí	22	0	0	36
Sonora	16	8	8	13
Veracruz	2	7	0	46
Total	--	--	--	327
Percent of total	11	12	5	--

Appendix Table 19

Publication of Books by Professors in Preceding Five Years

Faculty Type	Number of Professors Publishing: One Book	Two Books	Three Books or More	Total Number of Professors Publishing Books	Percentage of Professors Publishing Books	Number of Professors in Sample
Medical and dental sciences	7	6	8	21	39	56
Natural sciences	5	0	3	8	19	43
Architecture and engineering	14	1	4	19	26	73
Agronomy and veterinary medicine	2	2	2	6	24	25
Economics and business administration	13	5	3	21	29	71
Law and social sciences	0	1	1	2	7	31
Philosophy, humanities, and other	3	0	5	8	29	28
Total	44	15	26	85	--	327
Percent of total	--	--	--	--	26	--

University	Percentage of Professors Publishing at Least One Book
Guanajuato	14
Guadalajara	28
Estado de México	18
Michoacán	37
Nuevo León	16
Monterrey	51
San Luis Potosí	28
Sonora	38
Veracruz	11
Percent of total	26

Note: The category "books" includes published lecture notes or apuntes.

Appendix Table 20

Publication of Articles by Professors in Preceding Five Years

Faculty Type	Number of Professors Publishing: One or Two Articles	Three to Five Articles	More than Five Articles	Total Number of Professors Publishing Articles	Percentage of Professors Publishing Articles	Number of Professors in Sample
Medical and dental sciences	4	2	9	25	45	56
Natural sciences	4	2	2	8	19	43
Architecture and engineering	10	0	2	12	16	73
Agronomy and veterinary medicine	3	1	4	8	32	25
Economics and business administration	4	6	2	12	17	71
Law	2	2	2	6	19	31
Philosophy, humanities, and other	3	1	5	9	32	28
Total	30	14	26	80	--	327
Percent of total	--	--	--	--	24	--

University	Percentage of Professors Publishing at Least One Article
Guanajuato	24
Guadalajara	5
Estado de México	18
Michoacán	29
Nuevo León	27
Monterrey	34
San Luis Potosí	25
Sonora	38
Veracruz	24
Percent of total	24

Appendix Table 21

Membership of Professors in Professional Societies

Faculty Type	Number of Professors Belonging to			Total Number of Professors Belonging to Professional Societies	Number of Professors in Sample
	One Society	Two or Three Societies	More than Three Societies		
Medical and dental sciences	7	25	19	51	56
Natural sciences	11	14	2	27	43
Architecture and engineering	22	20	4	46	73
Agronomy and veterinary medicine	4	9	4	17	25
Economics and business administration	16	21	5	42	71
Law and social sciences	10	9	1	20	31
Philosophy, humanities, and other	8	4	3	15	28
Total	78	102	38	218	327

Note: F test for differences among faculty types: $p = .000$.
F test for differences among universities: $p = .78$ (not significant).

Table 22

Median Number of Hours Taught by Professors per Class per Week

Faculty Type	Median	10th Percen-tile	90th Percen-tile
Medical and dental sciences	5.0	2.0	12.0
Natural sciences	3.5	1.5	5.0
Architecture and engineering	4.3	2.5	7.0
Agronomy and veterinary medicine	3.0	2.0	5.0
Economics and business administration	3.3	2.5	5.0
Law	4.0	3.0	5.0
Philosophy	3.0	2.0	4.0

University	Median Hours per Class per Week
Guanajuato	4.3
Guadalajara	3.7
Estado de México	2.9
Michoacán	5.8
Nuevo León	3.6
Monterrey	2.3
San Luis Potosí	3.7
Sonora	2.9
Veracruz	3.6

Note: F test for differences among faculty types: $p = .000$.
F test for differences among universities: $p = .000$.

Appendix Table 23

Median Number of Hours of Laboratory Work by Professors per Class per Week

Faculty Type	Median	10th Percentile	90th Percentile
Medical and dental sciences	4.0	1.5	10.0
Natural sciences	3.0	1.0	8.0
Architecture and engineering	1.5	1.0	4.0
Agronomy and veterinary medicine	2.0	1.5	5.0

Note: F test: $p = .000$.

Appendix Table 24

Distribution of Total Contact Hours per Professor per Week, by Faculty Type

	Class Hours				Laboratory Hours				
	20th Percentile	Median	80th Percentile	Number of Professors Reporting	20th Percentile	Median	80th Percentile	Number of Professors Reporting	Number of Professors in Sample
Faculty type									
Medical and dental sciences	4	9	14	52	5	8	13	39	56
Natural sciences	6	10	13	42	4	6	13	26	43
Architecture and engineering	7	10	16	70	2	3	8	38	73
Agronomy and veterinary medicine	6	9	13	24	3	7	9	19	25
Economics and business administration	5	10	16	71	1	2	6	17	71
Law and social sciences	6	12	16	31	--	--	--	2	31
Philosophy, humanities, and other	5	11	15	28	--	--	--	2	28
Total	--	--	--	318	--	--	--	143	327
Overall	6	10	15	--	3	6	10	--	--
Hourly professors	4	8	13	157	3	6	10	50	163
Non-hourly professors	7	12	16	161	3	6	10	93	164
Total	--	--	--	318	--	--	--	143	327
Overall	6	10	15	--	3	6	10	--	--

Note: F test for differences among faculty types: $p = .34$ (not significant).

Appendix Table 25

Distribution of Total Contact Hours per Professor per Week, by University

	Class Hours				Laboratory Hours				
	20th Percentile	Median	80th Percentile	Number of Professors Reporting	20th Percentile	Median	80th Percentile	Number of Professors Reporting	Number of Professors in Sample
University									
Guanajuato	8	12	16	28	3	8	11	13	29
Guadalajara	7	10	16	40	3	7	13	14	40
Estado de México	3	8	15	21	1	3	12	5	22
Michoacán	9	13	17	24	4	7	9	16	24
Nuevo León	6	9	13	64	3	5	7	27	64
Monterrey	4	7	10	53	1	3	8	20	53
San Luis Potosí	5	10	16	34	2	4	13	22	36
Sonora	5	9	14	12	2	4	11	7	13
Veracruz	7	12	17	43	3	8	12	19	46
Total	--	--	--	318	--	--	--	143	327
Overall	6	10	15	--	3	6	10	--	--
Hourly professors	4	8	13	157	3	6	10	50	163
Non-hourly professors	7	12	16	161	3	6	10	93	164
Total	--	--	--	318	--	--	--	143	327
Overall	6	10	15	--	3	6	10	--	--

Note: F test among universities: p = .000.

Appendix Table 26

Estimated Total Number of Students Taught per Professor per Week

Faculty Type	20th Percentile	Median	80th Percentile	Number of Professors Reporting
Medical and dental sciences	40	80	150	56
Natural sciences	56	100	140	42
Architecture and engineering	44	90	120	72
Agronomy and veterinary medicine	60	100	155	23
Economics and business administration	41	110	180	71
Law and social sciences	70	160	240	30
Philosophy, humanities, and other	25	60	105	27
Total	--	--	--	321
Overall	50	100	140	--

University	Estimated Mean Value
Guanajuato	90
Guadalajara	190
Estado de México	80
Michoacán	130
Nuevo León	105
Monterrey	75
San Luis Potosí	100
Sonora	100
Veracruz	120
Overall	110

Note: F test among faculty types: p = .000.
F test among universities: p = .000 (mean values exceed median values because distribution is skewed).

Appendix Table 27

Distribution of Classes Taught by Professors by Year (Level)

Faculty Type	Percentage Distribution					Number of Classes Reported
	First Year	Second Year	Third Year	Fourth Year	Fifth Year and Up	
Medical and dental sciences	32	18	21	17	12	95
Natural sciences	28	27	22	20	3	104
Architecture and engineering	14	19	22	24	21	187
Agronomy and veterinary medicine	14	32	20	17	17	66
Economics and business administration	18	25	21	20	16	188
Law and social sciences	30	21	18	13	18	77
Philosophy, humanities, and other	19	28	25	14	14	43
Total	--	--	--	--	--	760
Percent of total	21	24	21	19	15	--

Appendix Table 28

Distribution of Class Size Reported by Professors

Faculty Type	10th Percentile	Median	90th Percentile	Number of Classes Reported
Medical and dental sciences	20	47	160	108
Natural sciences	6	36	55	134
Architecture and engineering	13	33	60	224
Agronomy and veterinary medicine	21	38	82	59
Economics and business administration	20	41	85	224
Law and social sciences	26	52	110	100
Philosophy, humanities, and other	7	15	40	106
Total	--	--	--	955
Overall	18	39	80	--

University	Estimated Mean Value
Guanajuato	35
Guadalajara	83
Estado de México	31
Michoacán	72
Nuevo León	46
Monterrey	30
San Luis Potosí	42
Sonora	34
Veracruz	45
Overall	46

Note: F test for means among faculty types: p = .000.
F test among universities: p = .000 (mean values exceed medians because of skewed distribution).

Appendix Table 29

Use of *Apuntes* (Professors' Notes)

Faculty Type	Percentage of Professors Using One Set of *Apuntes* or More per Course	Percentage of Professors Making Some Use of *Apuntes*	Number of Professors in Sample
Medical and dental sciences	10	29	56
Natural sciences	11	26	43
Architecture and engineering	27	56	73
Agronomy and veterinary medicine	20	44	25
Economics and business administration	10	47	71
Law and social sciences	20	36	31
Philosophy, humanities, and other	4	36	28
Total	--	--	327
Percent of total	15	39	--

Note: F test among faculty types: $p = .01$.
F test among universities: $p = .01$. (Lowest use of *apuntes* among universities was at the Technological Institute of Monterrey, where 26 percent of professors made some use of *apuntes*, and at Veracruz, where 33 percent of professors made some use of *apuntes*.)

Appendix Table 30

Required Use of Texts

Faculty Type	Spanish Texts		Non-Spanish Texts			
	Percentage of Professors Listing 1 or More per Course	Percentage of Professors Listing 2 or More per Course	Percentage of Professors Listing 1 or More per Course	Percentage of Professors Listing 2 or More per Course	Percentage of Professors Making Some Use of Texts*	Number of Professors in Sample
Medical and dental sciences	76	23	15	4	77	56
Natural sciences	36	5	38	2	86	43
Architecture and engineering	43	7	19	6	71	73
Agronomy and veterinary medicine	39	13	10	4	80	25
Economics and business administration	75	18	14	2	83	71
Law and social sciences	73	33	3	3	87	31
Philosophy, humanities, and other	52	20	14	5	71	28

*Response to question: "Do you use required texts in your courses?" (Other figures result from tally of texts listed in response to this question.)

Note: F test for use of Spanish texts among faculty types: $p = .000$.
F test for use of non-Spanish texts among faculty types: $p = .000$.
F test for use of Spanish texts among universities: $p = .20$.
F test for use of non-Spanish texts among universities: $p = .000$.
Among universities, the highest means for use of non-Spanish texts per course were .67 at the Technological Institute of Monterrey and .64 at Sonora. The overall mean for the use of non-Spanish texts per course for the 9 universities was .36.

Appendix Table 31

Required Use of Reference Books

Faculty Type	Spanish Reference Books		Non-Spanish Reference Books		Number of Professors in Sample
	Percentage of Professors Listing 1 or More per Course	Percentage of Professors Listing 2 or More per Course	Percentage of Professors Listing 1 or More per Course	Percentage of Professors Listing 2 or More per Course	
Medical and dental sciences	74	32	35	15	56
Natural sciences	44	12	64	29	43
Architecture and engineering	57	26	50	22	73
Agronomy and veterinary medicine	40	28	36	8	25
Economics and business administration	66	35	14	3	71
Law and social sciences	85	65	6	6	31
Philosophy, humanities, and other	57	40	5	--	28

Note: F test for use of Spanish reference books among faculty types: $p = .000$.
F test for use of non-Spanish reference books among faculty types: $p = .000$.
F test for use of Spanish reference books among universities: $p = .42$ (not significant).
F test for use of non-Spanish reference books among universities: $p = .01$.
Among universities, the highest means for the use of non-Spanish reference books per course were 1.8 at Sonora and 1.0 at the Technological Institute of Monterrey.

Appendix Table 32

Required Use of Journals

Faculty Type	Spanish Journals		Non-Spanish Journals		
	Percentage of Professors Listing 1 or More per Course	Percentage of Professors Listing 2 or More per Course	Percentage of Professors Listing 1 or More per Course	Percentage of Professors Listing 2 or More per Course	Number of Professors in Sample
Medical and dental sciences	16	5	18	11	56
Natural sciences	--	--	14	7	43
Architecture and engineering	8	--	8	7	73
Agronomy and veterinary medicine	4	4	24	8	25
Economics and business administration	14	9	9	5	71
Law and social sciences	26	10	--	--	31
Philosophy, humanities, and other	21	7	11	3	28

Note: F test for use of Spanish journals among faculty types: $p = .01$.
F test for use of non-Spanish journals among faculty types: $p = .01$.
F test for use of Spanish journals among universities: $p = .09$ (not significant).
F test for use of non-Spanish journals among universities: $p = .16$ (not significant).

Appendix Table 33

Use of Library Services by Professors
(percentage of professors using various central and faculty library services)

	Library	Medicine	Natural Sciences	Engineering and Architecture	Agriculture	Economics	Law	Philosophy	Total
Percentage receiving information on publications	Central	12	19	18	20	20	23	18	18
	Faculty	39	40	49	32	27	36	29	37
Percentage requesting publications	Central	5	20	8	30	14	23	17	14
	Faculty	50	26	45	38	28	26	17	33
Percentage reporting publications received	Central	2	14	8	24	12	20	10	11
	Faculty	40	16	37	38	24	15	10	30
Percentage using reserve shelves	Central	7	14	20	28	23	26	35	20
	Faculty	30	52	56	48	40	40	40	45

Appendix Table 34

Central and Faculty Library Services According to Professors, Directors, and Rectors

Service	Percentage Replying that Service Exists					
	Professors		Directors		Rectors	
	Central	Faculty	Central	Faculty	Central	Faculty
Information on new publications	18	37	25	44	83	n.a.
Reserve shelves	20	45	15	24	67	n.a.
Home circulation	n.a.	n.a.	22	46	50	n.a.
Acquisition of new books on professors' recommendation	24	50	32	64	83	n.a.

Appendix Table 35

Institutions Attended by Directors for Professional Degree, by University

Present University Affiliation	Number of Directors Attending				Number of Directors Reporting	Number of Directors in Sample
	Own Institution	UNAM	Autónoma de Guadalajara	Other		
Guanajuato	2	2	--	1	5	6
Guadalajara	1	1	2	3	7	11
Estado de México	1	5	--	2	8	8
Michoacán	2	1	1	--	4	4
Nuevo León	4	1	--	1	6	8
Monterrey	3	--	--	1	4	5
San Luis Potosí	5	2	--	1	8	8
Sonora	1	2	2	1	6	6
Veracruz	4	4	1	--	9	10
Total	23	18	6	10	57	66

Note: F test (attended present university, no-yes): $p = .047$.

Appendix Table 36

Institutions Attended by Directors for Professional Degree, by Faculty Type

Faculty Type	Number of Directors Attending					Number of Directors Reporting	Number of Directors in Sample
	UNAM	Monterrey and Nuevo León	Autónoma de Guadalajara	Other Mexico	Foreign		
Medical and dental sciences	4	--	1	3	--	8	11
Natural sciences	2	3	1	3	--	9	10
Architecture and engineering	6	3	1	5	--	15	16
Agronomy and veterinary medicine	1	--	--	2	--	3	4
Economics and business administration	2	2	--	5	--	9	11
Law and social sciences	2	1	1	3	--	7	7
Philosophy, humanities, and other	1	--	1	3	1	6	7
Total	18	9	5	24	1	57	66

Appendix Table 37

Distribution of Long and Short *Carreras* by Faculty Type (Directors' Questionnaire)

Faculty Type	Number of Faculties in Sample	Median Founding Date	Number of Long *Carreras*	Median Founding Date	Number of Short *Carreras*	Median Founding Date
Medical and dental sciences	11	1952	12	1962	2	1967
Natural sciences	10	1954	29	1965	2	1965
Architecture and engineering	16	1953	38	1965	6	1966
Agronomy and veterinary medicine	4	1953	10	1966	--	--
Economics and business administration	11	1949	19	1965	8	1964
Law and social sciences	7	1870	8	1962	3	n.a.
Philosophy, humanities, and other	7	1959	17	1966	1	n.a.

Appendix Table 38

Directors' Views of Future Directions of Cooperative Instructional Arrangements Outside Own Faculties

Response	Number of Directors in Favor
Support for present system	7
Joint courses and programs	14
Inter-faculty exchange of professors	4
Inter-institutional exchange of professors	5
Formation of departments	5
Exchange of physical resources	2
Cooperative research related to instruction	1
No response	28
Total	66

Appendix Table 39

Changes in the Professions as Seen by Directors

Type of Change	Medical and Dental Sciences	Natural Sciences	Architecture and Engineering	Agronomy and Veterinary Medicine	Economics and Business Administration	Law and Social Sciences	Philosophy, Humanities, and Other	Total
New social needs	1	--	1	--	1	--	--	3
New forms of public administration	--	--	1	--	3	--	--	4
Changes in social and economic demands	--	4	2	--	--	1	--	7
Methodological changes	--	7	6	--	2	--	1	16
General technical advances	--	--	5	2	1	--	1	9
New needs for specialization	--	2	1	--	1	1	--	5
Changes in hardware	--	2	3	--	4	--	--	9
There have been no changes	2	--	--	--	--	2	2	6
Total	3	15	19	2	12	4	4	59*
No response	9	3	6	2	3	4	4	31

*35 directors responded to this question and 24 of them gave 2 major changes; total number of responses is thus 59.

Appendix Table 40

Holdings of Faculty Libraries According to Deans
(figures in parentheses indicate number of deans reporting)

Faculty Type		Books		Journal Subscriptions in Spanish		Non-Spanish Journal Subscriptions		Number of Deans in Sample
Medical and dental sciences	80%ile	2,700	(9)	16	(6)	63	(5)	11
	Median	800		8		20		
	20%ile	200		4		4		
Natural sciences	80%ile	1,500	(9)	12	(7)	20	(8)	10
	Median	1,200		4		4		
	20%ile	400		2		2		
Architecture and engineering	80%ile	1,800	(14)	6	(11)	10	(11)	16
	Median	700		4		5		
	20%ile	300		2		2		
Agronomy and veterinary medicine	80%ile	*		*		*		
	Median	2,500	(3)	14	(3)	52	(3)	4
	20%ile	*		*		*		
Economics and business administration	80%ile	2,500	(7)	9	(8)	7	(8)	11
	Median	1,200		6		2		
	20%ile	1,000		2		0		
Law and social sciences	80%ile	7,000	(5)	15	(3)	4	(3)	7
	Median	5,000		8		0		
	20%ile	700		0		0		
Philosophy, humanities, and other	80%ile	3,000	(54)	11	(43)	15	(43)	56
	Median	1,300		4		4		
	20%ile	1,200		1		0		
Total	80%ile	3,000	(54)	11	(43)	15	(43)	56
	Median	1,300		4		4		
	20%ile	500		1		0		

*Insufficient data.

Note: F test among faculty types for holdings of books: p = .003.
F test among faculty types for journal subscriptions in Spanish: p = .49 (not significant).
F test among faculty types for non-Spanish journal subscriptions: p = .001.

Appendix Table 41

Library Services Provided by Central and Faculty Libraries

Service	Library	Medical	Natural Science	Engineering	Agronomy	Economics	Law	Philosophy	Total
Information on new publications	Central	4	2	5	1	4	1	--	17
	Faculty	2	2	11	2	6	3	3	29
Reserve shelves	Central	--	1	2	1	4	--	1	9
	Faculty	1	1	5	1	4	1	3	16
Home circulation	Central	1	3	4	1	5	--	2	16
	Faculty	6	6	7	2	4	2	5	32
Acquisitions for professors	Central	2	3	4	1	7	--	2	19
	Faculty	8	3	12	2	7	3	7	42
Total number of faculties in study		11	10	16	4	11	7	7	66

Appendix Table 42

Acquisitions Budgets of Faculty Libraries

Faculty Type	Number of Faculties Reporting Budgets for Acquisitions	Annual Median Budget (in dollars)
Medical and dental sciences	2	5,200
Natural sciences	5	1,000
Architecture and engineering	5	600
Agronomy and veterinary medicine	2	4,000
Economics and business administration	2	2,100
Law and social sciences	3	400
Philosophy, humanities, and other	3	1,800
Total	22	
Overall		1,300

Appendix Table 43

Acquisitions Budgets and Holdings of Central Libraries
(5 of 9 rectors reporting)

University	Holdings (number of volumes)	Annual Budget for Acquisitions (in dollars)
1	300,000	20,000
2	60,000	6,000
3	45,000	4,000
4	26,000	2,500
5	25,000	*

*No special budget for central library acquisitions.

Appendix Table 44

Faculty Library Staffs

Faculty Type	Median Number of Librarians and Assistants per Faculty	Percentage of Library Staff Working Full Time	Median Monthly Salary (in dollars)	Percentage of Library Staff with Some University Training	Number of Faculties Reporting
Medical and dental sciences	3	37	100	25	9/11
Natural sciences	1	37	100	63	9/10
Architecture and engineering	2	60	100	50	13/16
Agronomy and veterinary medicine	1	50	150	50	2/4
Economics and business administration	1.5	37	100	13	8/11
Law and social sciences	2	67	150	44	6/7
Philosophy, humanities, and other	1	50	100	50	6/7
Total	--	--	--	--	53/66
Overall	1	50	100+	40	--

Appendix Table 45

Directors' Opinions on Most Important Changes in Libraries

Change	In Faculty Library in Preceding 5 Years	In Central Library in Preceding 5 Years	In Faculty Library in the Future
Improvement in professional service (personnel)	1	2	8
Improvement in organization	5	1	6
Improvement in cataloging	16	3	7
Better coordination between faculty and central libraries	1	1	3
Special services: e.g., bibliography, microfilm, Xerox	2	--	3
Physical improvements	13	2	13
Increase in acquisitions	20	2	37
Increase in budget or outside funding	1	--	4
No change or reduction in service	11	6	2
Don't know	--	11	--
Total	70	28	83

Appendix Table 46

Methods of Recruitment of Professors
(numbers indicate affirmative responses by deans)

Faculty Type	Recruiting Program	Correspondence with Other Universities	Publicity in Professional Publications	Correspondence with Professional Associations	Personal Visits	Recruitment of Own Best Graduates	Number of Faculties in Study
Medicine	7	4	3	2	3	9	11
Natural sciences	7	5	1	4	4	6	10
Engineering	8	8	3	6	9	9	16
Agronomy	2	1	1	1	1	1	4
Economics	5	4	2	2	4	9	11
Law	7	3	1	2	2	5	7
Philosophy	2	--	--	1	2	4	7
Total	38	25	11	18	25	43	66

Note: F tests among both faculty types and universities showed no significant differences.

Appendix Table 47

Total Enrollments in Individual Faculties in 1967

	Mean	Median	Standard Deviation	Number of Faculties in Sample
Faculty type				
Medicine	559	280	480	11/11
Natural sciences	256	194	212	10/10
Engineering	422	284	430	17/17
Agriculture	267	237	159	6/6
Economics	811	548	657	13/13
Law	719	571	479	8/8
Philosophy	201	174	143	6/6
Total group	493	291	477	71/71
University				
Guanajuato	322	152	490	11/11
Guadalajara	926	735	675	7/7
Estado de México	208	157	128	7/7
Michoacán	457	467	372	7/7
Nuevo León	578	504	409	11/11
Monterrey	813	517	816	5/5
San Luis Potosí	313	315	164	8/8
Sonora	294	291	135	5/5
Veracruz	590	417	464	10/10
Total group	493	291	477	71/71

Appendix Table 48

Percentage Gain in Enrollment in Individual Faculties, 1961-67

	Mean	Median	Standard Deviation	Number of Faculties in Sample
Faculty type				
Medicine	109	123	64	10/11
Natural sciences	205	208	206	9/10
Engineering	65	28	80	13/17
Agriculture	193	160	130	4/6
Economics	290	186	302	12/13
Law	95	92	60	8/8
Philosophy	200	176	157	4/6
Total group	160	120	184	60/71
University				
Guanajuato	173	55	348	10/11
Guadalajara	185	184	44	6/7
Estado de México	112	97	117	4/7
Michoacán	175	127	108	4/7
Nuevo León	112	31	134	11/11
Monterrey	74	74	58	4/5
San Luis Potosí	166	178	76	8/8
Sonora	235	146	254	5/5
Veracruz	199	139	186	8/10
Total group	160	120	184	60/71

Appendix Table 49

Changes in Relative Standing of Faculties According to Enrollments, 1961-67

	1961 Relative Standing			1967 Relative Standing			Change in Standing 1961-67			
	In Mean Standard Deviation	In Median Standard Deviation	Number of Faculties Reporting	In Mean Standard Deviation	In Median Standard Deviation	Number of Faculties Reporting	In Mean Standard Deviation	In Median Standard Deviation	Number of Faculties Reporting	Number of Faculties in Sample
Faculty type										
Medicine	.206	−.227	10	.138	−.446	11	.034	.070	10	11
Natural sciences	−.535	−.710	9	−.497	−.635	10	.062	−.007	9	10
Engineering	.244	−.349	13	−.148	−.437	17	−.307	−.205	13	17
Agronomy	−.492	−.553	4	−.473	−.535	6	.171	.155	4	6
Economics	.020	−.261	12	.667	.116	13	.759	.395	12	13
Law	.491	.089	8	.475	.165	8	−.016	.018	8	8
Philosophy	−.653	−.757	4	−.611	−.668	6	.125	.173	4	6
University										
Guanajuato	−.525	−.533	10	−.357	−.714	11	.219	−.015	10	11
Guadalajara	.445	.492	6	.907	.507	7	.722	.675	6	7
Estado de México	−.445	−.511	4	−.597	−.703	7	.005	.002	4	7
Michoacán	−.144	−.292	4	−.074	−.054	7	.245	.183	4	7
Nuevo León	.622	.559	10	.180	.023	11	−.442	−.404	11	11
Monterrey	1.208	.822	4	.670	.051	5	−.158	.027	4	5
San Luis Potosí	−.489	−.418	8	−.377	−.372	8	.112	.092	8	8
Sonora	−.540	−.469	5	−.416	−.423	5	.124	.101	5	5
Veracruz	−.013	−.221	8	.204	−.159	10	.440	.232	8	10

Appendix Table 50

Overall Retention Rates
(percentages)

	Mean	Median	Standard Deviation	Number of Faculties Reporting
<u>Faculty type</u>				
Medicine	51	50	16	10/11
Natural sciences	42	41	24	10/10
Engineering	51	53	23	13/17
Agriculture	57	58	19	4/6
Economics	56	52	16	11/13
Law	63	56	17	8/8
Philosophy	31	29	13	4/6
Total group	51	50	20	60/71
<u>University</u>				
Guanajuato	49	49	22	9/11
Guadalajara	48	47	12	6/7
Estado de México	23	23	7	2/7
Michoacán	59	59	15	5/7
Nuevo León	52	56	21	11/11
Monterrey	n.a.	n.a.	n.a.	0/5
San Luis Potosí	56	62	31	8/8
Sonora	53	44	27	5/5
Veracruz	51	53	14	9/10
Total group	51	50	20	60/71

Note: Retention rates were computed by following first year enrollments in 1961 and 1962 through to fourth, fifth, or sixth year enrollments in 1966 and 1967 (depending on length of professional program).

Appendix Table 51

Percentage of Full-time Professors per Faculty

	Mean	Median	Standard Deviation	Number of Faculties Reporting
Faculty type				
Medicine	05	05	04	9/11
Natural sciences	25	25	23	10/10
Engineering	16	14	15	17/17
Agriculture	35	40	30	6/6
Economics	13	06	13	13/13
Law	06	05	07	8/8
Philosophy	14	12	13	6/6
Total group	16	09	18	69/71
University				
Guanajuato	05	03	07	10/11
Guadalajara	09	08	06	5/7
Estado de México	06	07	04	5/7
Michoacán	07	06	06	7/7
Nuevo León	26	30	15	10/11
Monterrey	43	44	17	5/5
San Luis Potosí	07	05	08	8/8
Sonora	30	28	25	5/5
Veracruz	21	15	23	10/10
Total group	16	09	18	69/71

Appendix Table 52

Percentage of Faculty Budget Spent on Professors' Salaries

	Mean	Median	Standard Deviation	Number of Faculties Reporting
Faculty type				
Medicine	60	55	13	11/11
Natural sciences	70	75	13	10/10
Engineering	71	75	17	16/17
Agriculture	50	53	15	6/6
Economics	68	72	12	12/13
Law	74	76	14	7/8
Philosophy	79	77	11	6/6
Total group	68	72	15	68/71
University				
Guanajuato	83	87	14	9/11
Guadalajara	53	50	16	6/7
Estado de México	72	79	14	7/7
Michoacán	73	79	16	7/7
Nuevo León	73	74	08	11/11
Monterrey	56	45	22	5/5
San Luis Potosí	64	69	12	8/8
Sonora	60	62	07	5/5
Veracruz	64	67	11	10/10
Total group	68	72	15	68/71

Appendix Table 53

Average Number of Hours of Use
per Classroom per Week

	Mean	Median	Standard Deviation	Number of Faculties Reporting
Faculty type				
Medicine	42	37	25	4/11
Natural sciences	30	30	8	2/10
Engineering	23	27	15	8/17
Agriculture	20	20	0	1/6
Economics	26	24	5	5/13
Law	33	33	15	2/8
Philosophy	33	33	4	2/6
Total group	29	29	15	24/71
University				
Guanajuato	n.a.	n.a.	n.a.	--/11
Guadalajara	n.a.	n.a.	n.a.	--/7
Estado de México	31	30	09	7/7
Michoacán	21	24	10	4/7
Nuevo León	n.a.	n.a.	n.a.	--/11
Monterrey	n.a.	n.a.	n.a.	--/5
San Luis Potosí	34	29	14	3/8
Sonora	28	30	06	3/5
Veracruz	29	20	24	7/10
Total group	29	29	15	24/71

Appendix Table 54

Total Expenditures per Student per Faculty in 1967
(in dollars)

	Mean	Median	Standard Deviation	Number of Faculties Reporting
Faculty type				
Medicine	290	240	16	11/11
Natural sciences	600	290	72	10/10
Engineering	304	250	16	16/17
Agriculture	384	360	22	6/6
Economics	144	112	112	12/13
Law	92	96	35	7/8
Philosophy	416	336	280	6/6
Total group	314	230	356	68/71
University				
Guanajuato	280	240	184	9/11
Guadalajara	144	160	200	6/7
Estado de México	344	336	160	7/7
Michoacán	123	118	40	7/7
Nuevo León	328	296	168	11/11
Monterrey	1,064	734	960	5/5
San Luis Potosí	146	154	64	8/8
Sonora	372	438	230	5/5
Veracruz	272	240	198	10/10
Total group	314	230	356	68/71

Note: Expenditures were computed using total 1967 expenditure and total (not full-time equivalent) 1967 enrollment.

Appendix Table 55

Percentage of Enrollment from Within State in Which Faculty Is Located

	Mean	Median	Standard Deviation	Number of Faculties Reporting
Faculty type				
Medicine	80	77	7	4/11
Natural sciences	70	75	24	4/10
Engineering	79	90	25	6/17
Agriculture	63	65	25	5/6
Economics	75	83	22	7/13
Law	83	83	7	4/8
Philosophy	77	74	13	4/6
Total group	75	79	20	34/71
University				
Guanajuato	n.a.	n.a.	n.a.	--
Guadalajara	68	69	6	7/7
Estado de México	85	85	8	2/7
Michoacán	84	83	7	7/7
Nuevo León	n.a.	n.a.	n.a.	--
Monterrey	38	35	17	5/5
San Luis Potosí	n.a.	n.a.	n.a.	--
Sonora	86	90	7	5/5
Veracruz	87	90	12	8/10
Total group	75	79	20	34/71

Appendix Table 56

Factor Analysis of Professors' Responses
(standardized weights for principal components)

Variable Description	Variable Number	Factor Number					
		1	2	3	4	5	6
Faculty type	1	.32	−.01	−.62	−.10	.05	.01
Teacher category, non-hourly/hourly	2	.28	−.35	−.04	−.43	.11	.05
Number of courses professor teaches	3	.08	.26	−.34	.66	.11	−.05
Number of class hours per week	4	−.16	−.17	−.40	.68	−.08	−.04
Number of lab hours per week	5	−.50	.02	.53	.02	.31	−.01
Number of hours consulting with students	6	−.11	.30	.03	.30	−.01	−.16
Grand total hours	7	−.19	−.06	.11	.17	.27	−.05
Type of outside job	8	.03	−.23	−.11	−.38	.18	.09
Uses notes, no-yes	9	−.12	−.23	−.17	−.24	.42	−.23
Requires journals, no-yes	10	−.30	.34	−.23	−.13	.24	−.19
Central library, no-yes	11	−.15	.43	−.12	−.26	−.13	.04
Central library orders books, no-yes	12	.08	.44	−.21	−.29	−.21	.10
Central library publications requested	13	.04	.43	−.19	−.31	−.20	.12
Central library publications acquired	14	.07	.42	−.18	−.30	−.21	.12
Central reserve books, no-yes	15	.11	.49	−.21	−.24	−.15	.02
Requires essays, no-yes	16	.07	.25	−.20	−.06	.35	−.04
Secondary school same state, no-yes	17	.28	−.40	.25	−.08	−.00	−.09
Preparatoria same state, no-yes	18	.30	−.31	.28	−.04	−.05	−.14
University same state, no-yes	19	.41	−.30	.37	.02	−.01	−.08
Preparatoria public-private	20	.28	.30	−.01	−.07	−.04	−.09

Preparatory year of graduation	21	.38	−.04	.05	.11	.06	−.43
University public-private	22	.34	.39	.08	−.01	−.11	−.11
Graduate of present university, no-yes	23	.41	−.30	.41	.09	−.04	−.08
Graduate of UNAM or Monterrey, no-yes	24	.54	.22	.29	.07	.01	.00
University year of graduation	26	.39	−.00	.09	.08	.03	−.42
Post-graduate training in same state, no-yes	27	.66	−.02	.15	.11	.28	.30
Post-graduate training in present university, no-yes	28	.65	.00	.14	.08	.27	.38
Post-graduate training at UNAM or Monterrey, no-yes	29	.67	.08	.23	.03	.24	.34
Post-graduate title	31	−.21	.15	.07	−.13	−.19	−.20
Year post-graduate degree received	32	.45	−.00	.11	.11	.08	−.29
English fluency, low-high	33	−.11	.28	.06	.04	−.03	−.03
Number of languages known	34	−.24	.26	−.13	.02	−.10	.13
Number of subjects taught	35	.09	.44	−.20	.02	.03	.07
Number of books written	36	−.26	.16	.01	.04	−.10	.57
Number of articles written	37	−.23	.22	.09	.03	−.06	.50
Number of unpublished researches	38	−.27	.10	.10	.03	.02	.50
Number of professional society memberships	39	−.35	.13	.14	.03	−.03	.39
Number of consulting jobs	40	.11	.14	−.20	−.24	.03	.22
Number of changes in profession listed	41	.07	.33	−.09	−.11	.04	.10
Quality of response to changes in profession, low-high	42	.00	.34	.05	−.07	.11	.10
Quality of response to changes in program, low-high	43	.02	.46	.08	.05	.13	−.01
Average hours per class	44	−.25	−.34	−.04	.12	−.12	.03
Total hours class	45	−.11	−.12	−.44	.71	−.06	−.02
Average hours laboratory	46	−.45	−.03	.56	−.15	.24	−.02
Total hours laboratory	47	−.49	.04	.53	.02	.32	.03
Average number of students	48	−.25	−.35	.21	.15	−.03	.25
Total number of students	49	−.15	−.16	−.07	.63	.04	.23
Average number of assistants	50	−.38	−.04	.47	−.03	.10	.17
Total number of assistants	51	−.36	.09	.43	.17	.11	.20
Average number of Spanish texts	52	−.16	−.24	−.12	−.17	.30	.05

(continued)

Appendix Table 56 (continued)

Variable Description	Variable Number	Factor Number					
		1	2	3	4	5	6
Total number of Spanish texts	53	−.14	−.07	−.30	.21	.39	.02
Average number of texts, other languages	54	.11	.51	.34	.15	.00	−.14
Total number of texts, other languages	55	.11	.55	.21	.31	−.03	−.13
Average number of notes	56	−.21	−.07	.02	−.26	.41	−.22
Total number of notes	57	−.16	−.02	−.14	−.11	.54	−.27
Average number of Spanish reference books	58	.02	−.29	−.14	−.20	.19	.21
Total number of Spanish reference books	59	.01	−.16	−.35	.19	.28	.17
Average number of reference books, other languages	60	−.07	.32	.40	.12	−.05	−.26
Total number of reference books, other languages	61	−.00	.37	.29	.36	−.07	−.24
Average number of Spanish journals	62	−.13	−.04	−.21	−.18	.31	−.24
Total number of Spanish journals	63	−.13	.05	−.28	−.03	.34	−.25
Average number of journals, other languages	64	−.32	.32	.27	−.09	.13	−.22
Total number of journals, other languages	65	−.28	.44	.06	.04	.15	−.23
Average number of essays	66	.09	.17	−.09	.00	.59	.13
Total number of essays	67	.10	.24	−.17	.10	.60	.06
Average number pages per course	68	.11	.21	.02	.02	.37	.15
Total pages all courses	69	.13	.23	−.14	.09	.37	.15
Latent roots		5.95	4.99	4.34	3.59	3.38	3.09

Appendix Table 57

Factor Analysis of Directors' Variables
(standardized weights for principal components)

Variable Description	Variable Number	Factor Number			
		1	2	3	4
Year school founded	1	.18	−.23	−.25	.16
Long _carrera_, date established	2	−.11	.05	.37	−.20
Number long _carreras_	3	.02	.22	−.27	−.18
Number short _carreras_	4	−.10	−.27	−.05	−.27
Short _carrera_, date established	5	.23	−.22	−.03	−.39
Other cooperating faculties	6	−.57	−.09	.36	.33
Number of cooperative programs	7	−.57	.11	.28	−.11
Number of types of faculty cooperation	8	−.61	−.12	.21	−.01
Quality of response, types of cooperation	9	−.74	−.08	.13	.30
Number of changes in profession listed	10	−.60	.24	.09	−.38
Quality of response, changes in profession	11	−.64	.02	.05	−.29
Program changes	12	−.44	.26	.21	−.44
Number of changes in school	13	−.40	.37	.06	−.31
Quality of response, changes in school	14	−.52	.33	.08	−.38
Number of institutional cooperative arrangements	15	−.45	−.06	−.07	−.22
Number researches related to instruction	16	−.22	−.46	−.02	−.12
Number researches unrelated to instruction	17	.10	.06	−.41	.08
Quality of response, research	18	−.25	−.02	−.46	−.18
Quality of response, research related to instruction	19	−.42	−.07	−.14	−.11
Research with other institutions	20	−.38	−.01	−.23	−.14

(continued)

Appendix Table 57 (continued)

Variable Description	Variable Number	Factor Number 1	2	3	4
Years research program in progress	21	−.29	.02	.53	.16
How research funded	22	.12	.23	.05	−.33
Incentives to professors for research, no-yes	23	−.53	.01	−.15	.41
How long established	24	−.16	−.34	−.20	.26
Community courses, no-yes	25	−.69	−.04	−.02	.25
Quality of response, community courses	26	−.62	−.04	−.01	.43
How long established	27	−.24	.02	−.31	.37
Faculty improvement program, no-yes	28	−.33	−.02	.19	.07
How long faculty improvement program	29	−.27	−.05	.42	.28
Quality of response, faculty improvement program	30	−.51	−.04	.10	−.09
Number professors in program	31	−.06	.11	−.43	−.00
Economic incentives to self-development	32	−.61	−.15	.26	.01
Quality of response, economic incentives	33	−.60	−.15	.27	.07
Central library, no-yes	34	−.31	−.04	−.33	−.19
Sum central library services	35	−.70	−.01	−.44	−.04
Use of central library subscriptions, no-yes	36	−.56	−.06	−.23	.05
Quality of response, central subscriptions	37	−.71	.13	−.46	−.11
Number of volumes, faculty library	38	.14	−.41	−.10	.13
Number of Spanish subscriptions, faculty library	39	.02	−.14	.05	.17
Number of other subscriptions, faculty library	40	−.28	−.47	−.14	.32

Size of reading room, faculty library	41	.08	−.00	−.03	.23
Sum bibliography service, faculty library	42	.06	−.58	.15	.04
Special budget, faculty library	43	.14	−.58	.15	.04
Budget-1,000s, faculty library	44	.06	−.22	−.12	.20
Number of assistants, faculty library	45	.15	−.60	−.17	−.03
Library assistants, type appointment, faculty library	46	−.15	.55	.04	.39
Educational background, faculty library assistants	47	−.11	−.33	.22	.02
Sum changes, faculty library	48	.05	−.54	.28	−.13
Central library changes	49	−.53	.10	.04	−.08
Sum future library plans, faculty library	50	.12	−.50	−.08	−.13
Budgetary needs of professors considered, no-yes	51	−.07	−.06	−.07	.01
Number of budget changes proposed	52	−.22	−.31	−.21	−.48
Recruiting system for professors, no-yes	53	−.16	−.00	−.36	.08
Number of methods of recruitment	54	−.44	−.03	−.15	.08
New methods suggested, no-yes	55	−.09	−.15	−.44	.26
Proposed change in recruiting system, no-yes	56	.03	−.26	−.02	−.37
Promotion system for professors, no-yes	57	.14	.40	−.23	−.02
How long in effect	58	.09	.24	.17	−.10
Geographic restrictions on admission, no-yes	59	−.14	.01	.00	−.05
Number of course failures allowed	60	.26	−.17	.24	−.03
Advising available, no-yes	61	.36	−.10	.02	.11
Placement program, no-yes	62	−.45	−.21	−.26	.12
Advising program, no-yes	63	−.29	−.32	.28	−.09
Faculty role-university plan, no-yes	64	−.15	−.23	−.33	−.18
Deans' post-graduate institution same as present, no-yes	65	−.01	−.04	.42	.16
Year first professional degree received	66	−.12	−.44	.24	−.33
Number courses dean teaches	67	.23	.21	−.02	−.34
Latent roots		8.97	4.47	3.89	3.55

Appendix Table 58

Correlations of Professors' Responses with Criterion Variables and Regression Analyses

	Overall Retention (Monterrey omitted)
Faculty type (science/non-science)	—.07
Appointments (non-hourly/hourly)	.05
Number of courses taught	—.15
Number of class hours per week	.00
Number of lab hours per week	—.07
Number of university office hours per week	.03
Use of <u>apuntes</u> (no-yes)	—.08
Central university library (no-yes)	—.03
Number of publications ordered from central library	—.06
Number of publications acquired from central library	—.02
Use of central library reserve shelves	—.08
Require essays (no-yes)	—.08
Attended secondary school in same state (no-yes)	.10
Attended preparatory school in same state (no-yes)	.13
Attended university in same state (no-yes)	.17
University attended is public-private	—.02
Attended present university (yes-no)	.14
Attended UNAM or Monterrey (no-yes)	.36
English fluency (low-high)	.01
Number of professional society memberships	.15
Changes in profession (quality of response)	—.04
Changes in courses (quality of response)	—.09
Total hours of class	.00
Average hours lab per course	—.04
Total hours lab per week	—.06
Average number of students per course	.38
Total number of students per week	.27
Average number of assistants per course	.23
Average number of Spanish texts per course	.07
Total number of Spanish texts used	—.03
Total number of texts in other languages	—.11
Total number of <u>apuntes</u>	—.05
Average number of Spanish reference books per course	.15
Total number of Spanish reference books used	.16
Average number of reference books, other languages	—.10
Multiple R	
R^2	

Beta Weights	Relative Rate of Growth of Enrollments per School	Beta Weights	Estimate of Quality of Faculty Type	Beta Weights	Estimate of Quality of University	Beta Weights
	.30	.34	--		.11	
.11	.01		−.10		−.15	
−.31	.05		−.25		.03	
	.07		−.06		−.20	
	−.03		.41	.25	−.15	
	−.06		.08		.23	.15
	.02		−.01		−.17	−.12
	.02		−.04		.15	
	−.02		−.10		.19	
	−.03		−.10		.19	
	−.11	−.10	−.15		.30	.12
	−.04		−.15		.01	
	.12		−.03		−.08	
	.11	.16	−.02		.01	
	.02		−.04		.08	.25
	−.11		−.08		.28	
	−.01		−.01		−.02	.64
.40	−.37	−.37	−.05		.59	.64
	−.14		.15		.16	
	−.02		.28	.21	.01	
	−.05		.08		.08	
	−.12		.17	.15	.13	
	.12		−.11		−.20	−.12
	−.07		.36		−.15	
	−.03		.38		−.16	
.12	.25	.26	.09		−.12	
.42	.25		−.08		−.08	
	−.20	−.13	.43	.28	−.02	
	.02		−.13		−.16	
	.09		−.27	−.18	−.15	
	−.17		.09		.22	
	−.02		−.05		−.09	
	−.01	−.13	−.19		−.04	
	−.01		−.33	−.26	.01	
	−.17		.20		.16	
.60		.60		.67		.72
.36		.36		.44		.52
N=274		N=327		N=327		N=327

Appendix Table 59

Correlations of Directors' Responses with Criterion Variables and Regression Analyses

		Overall Reten-tion (Mon-terrey omitted)
1	Faculty type (science/non-science)	.19
2	Year school founded	.03
4	Number of short carreras	.03
5	Number of cooperating faculties	—.26
6	Number of cooperative instructional arrangements	—.29
7	Number of positive opinions on faculty cooperation	—.26
8	Quality of response on inter-faculty cooperation	—.22
9	Number of changes in profession cited	—.04
10	Quality of response on changes in profession	.00
11	Program changes (no-yes)	.08
12	Number of program changes in school	—.08
13	Quality of response on changes in school	—.07
14	Number of external cooperative arrangements	—.12
15	Number of researches related to instruction	—.30
16	Number of researches unrelated to instruction	—.21
17	Quality of response on research	—.33
18	Quality of response on research in instruction	—.22
19	Research with other institution (no-yes)	—.27
22	Incentives to professors for research (no-yes)	—.17
23	Community courses (no-yes)	—.12
24	Quality of response on community courses	.03
25	Faculty improvement program (no-yes)	—.03
27	Quality of response on faculty improvement program	—.08
28	Incentives to professors for promotion (no-yes)	—.14
29	Quality of response on promotion of professors	—.12

Beta Weights	Relative Rate of Growth of Enroll-ments per School	Beta Weights	Esti-mate of Quality of Faculty Type	Beta Weights	Esti-mate of Quality of Uni-versity	Beta Weights
	.16		--		.03	
	—.33	—.48	.00		—.12	
	.36	.48	.01		.15	
—.30	—.20		.19		.14	
	—.02		.08		.03	
	—.17		.07		.26	
	—.16		.23		.11	
	.23		—.07	—.36	.13	
	.15	.29	.02		.24	.25
	.19		—.04		.00	
	.11		.12		—.07	
	.09		.03		—.04	
	—.04		.14		—.15	—.32
	.04		—.22		.20	
	—.02		.15		—.04	
—.25	—.01		.03		—.05	
	—.02		.01		.06	
	—.10		.23		—.01	
	—.24		.25	.24	.23	
	.00		.15		.27	
	—.02		.19		—.35	.25
	—.01		—.04		.08	
	—.12	—.21	.16		.04	
	—.28	—.50	.37	.35	.31	.25
	—.31		.29		.30	

(continued)

Appendix Table 59 (continued)

		Overall Retention (Monterrey omitted)
30	Central library (no-yes)	.14
31	Sum of central library services	-.15
32	Does faculty use central library publications (no-yes)	-.23
33	Quality of response on central subscriptions	-.11
34	Number of volumes in faculty library	-.14
37	Sum of bibliographic services in faculty library	-.14
38	Special budget for faculty library (no-yes)	.06
40	Library assistant, type of appointment (hourly-full)	.06
42	Sum of changes, faculty library	-.14
43	Central library changes	-.08
47	Number of methods of recruitment	-.38
48	Other recruitment methods	.09
49	Recruitment plans for change	.23
50	Promotion system (no-yes)	-.06
51	Years promotion system in effect	.00
52	Geographical restrictions on administration (no-yes)	-.08
53	Number of course failures allowed per year	.20
54	Advising system (no-yes)	-.20
55	Placement program (no-yes)	-.07
56	Information on post-graduate programs (no-yes)	.07
57	Faculty role in university planning (no-yes)	.28
58	Dean post-graduate studies at present institution (no-yes)	.32
59	Year post-graduate degree	-.18
60	Number of courses dean teaches	.13
	Multiple R	
	R^2	

Beta Weights	Relative Rate of Growth of Enroll-ments per School	Beta Weights	Esti-mate of Quality of Faculty Type	Beta Weights	Esti-mate of Quality of Uni-versity	Beta Weights
.24	.27		−.06		.11	
	.07		.02		.14	
	−.05		.05		.22	
	.15		−.07		.11	
	−.08		−.40	−.46	.27	.33
−.22	−.12		−.00		.05	
	−.01		−.03		.14	
	−.03		−.21	−.21	.11	
	−.36	−.31	−.02		.10	
	−.14		−.07		.04	
−.30	.03		.02		.05	
	−.16		.08		.06	
	.01		−.06		.09	
	.23		.09		−.23	
	.05		.18		.11	
	−.03		−.21		.14	
.22	−.15		−.15		.19	
	−.07		.01		−.04	
	.08		−.04		.25	
	.00		−.09		.20	
.34	−.06		−.14		.01	
.23	−.14		−.14	−.25	.15	
	.15		−.11		.11	
	.28		−.10		−.19	
.74		.80		.69		.60
.55		.64		.48		.36
N=61		N=66		N=66		N=66

Appendix Table 60

Regression Analyses of Certain Activities Indexes Based on Directors' Responses

		Index of Inter-Faculty Coop-eration	Beta Weights
2	Year school founded	—.01	
3	Year major carrera founded	.22	
4	Number of short carreras	.00	
14	Number of external cooperative arrangements	.38	.29
22	Incentives to research (no-yes)	.35	
37	Sum of bibliographical services (faculty library)	—.24	
38	Budget for faculty library (no-yes)	.04	
39	Number of assistants in faculty library	—.03	
40	Library assistant, type of appointment	.21	.30
41	Size of library reading room	.21	
42	Sum of changes, faculty library	.11	
43	Central library changes	.41	.31
44	Sum future library plans	.00	
45	Number of budget changes proposed	.08	
46	Recruiting system (no-yes)	.11	
47	Number of methods of recruitment	.31	
48	New methods of recruitment	—.05	
49	Planned changes in recruitment	—.06	
50	Promotion system (no-yes)	—.08	
53	Number of course failures allowed per year	—.11	
54	Advising system (no-yes)	.19	
55	Placement program (no-yes)	.18	
56	Information on post-graduate programs (no-yes)	.24	.29
57	Faculty role in university planning (no-yes)	.10	
58	Dean post-graduate degree at present institution	.01	
59	Year dean obtained degree	.15	
60	Number of courses dean teaches	—.33	—.30
61	Overall retention	—.32	—.26
62	Total 1967 registration	—.12	
67	Relative gain in enrollment (1961-67)	—.17	
	Multiple R		.74
	R^2		.55

Index of Program Change	Beta Weights	Index of Research	Beta Weights	Index of Community Courses	Beta Weights	Index of Staff Development	Beta Weights
−.25		.05		−.03		−.25	−.33
.18	.33	−.09		.10		.03	
.01		.01		.15	.24	.14	
.25	.16	.31		.22		.31	
.17		.25		.51	.42	.34	.29
−.22		.06		−.13		.22	.22
−.20		−.02		−.06		−.04	
−.30	−.31	.09		−.18	−.35	−.08	
.10		.03		.13		−.02	
.03		.02		.03		.05	
−.10		.15		−.14		−.01	
.26		.10		−.17		−.08	
−.19		.10		−.17		−.08	
.22	.29	.29		−.07		.06	
.01		.38	.31	.02		−.02	
.22	.25	.28		.20		.36	.28
−.16		.16		.18		−.08	
.10		−.07		.02		−.09	
.10		.16		−.13		−.09	
−.05		.05		−.15		.04	
.23		.38	.29	.19		.15	
.13		.22		.29		.24	
.15		−.03		.19	.26	.25	
.04		.18	.21	.11		−.02	
.11	.21	−.28		.05		.05	
.05		−.03		.06		.10	
.06		−.04		−.44	−.39	−.07	
−.03		−.35	−.32	−.08		−.14	
.24	.38	−.19		.09		.03	
.16		−.05		−.01		−.24	−.26
	.65		.61		.73		.63
	.43		.37		.54		.39

Appendix Table 61

Inter-correlations of Directors' Activity Indexes

Variable Description	Variable Number	Variable Number					
		89	90	91	92	93	94
Inter-faculty cooperation index	89	1.000	.340**	.220	.518**	.491**	.276*
Program change index	90	.340**	1.000	.216	.214	.149	.268*
Research index	91	.220	.216	1.000	.213	.066	.207
Community courses index	92	.518**	.214	.213	1.000	.361**	.423**
Staff development index	93	.491**	.149	.066	.361**	1.000	.338**
Central library index	94	.276*	.269*	.207	.423**	.338**	1.000

*Significant at .05 level.
**Significant at .01 level.

Appendix Table 62

Discriminant Analysis of Professors' Responses: Standardized Coefficients for First Four Discriminants

Variable Number	Row	Variable Description	Discriminant 1	2	3	4
1	1	Faculty type	0.21	0.16	−0.09	0.10
2	2	Teacher category	−0.23	0.30	0.09	−0.07
3	3	Courses	0.03	−0.01	−0.10	−0.33
6	4	Hours of consultation	0.14	−0.07	0.34	0.17
9	5	Use of notes	−0.18	−0.09	0.10	0.12
14	6	Central reserve books	0.53	0.07	0.15	0.25
15	7	Requires essays	0.05	0.23	−0.15	0.23
16	8	Attended secondary school in same state	−0.05	−0.33	0.13	0.26
17	9	Attended preparatory school in same state	−0.18	−0.42	−0.18	−0.18
18	10	Attended university in same state	0.12	0.39	0.67	−0.23
30	11	English fluency	0.30	−0.09	0.05	−0.13
64	12	Number of articles published	0.01	−0.09	0.19	−0.10
35	13	Quality of response, profession changes	0.04	0.27	−0.37	−0.22
36	14	Quality of response, program changes	0.05	0.02	−0.17	−0.01
37	15	Total hours class	−0.50	−0.08	0.09	0.49
39	16	Total hours laboratory	−0.17	0.04	0.04	0.35
40	17	Average number of students	−0.32	0.24	0.15	0.21
41	18	Total number of students	0.04	0.43	−0.03	−0.14
42	19	Average number of assistants	−0.00	−0.02	0.02	−0.19
45	20	Non-Spanish texts	0.17	−0.08	0.22	0.13
47	21	Reference books (Spanish)	−0.02	−0.15	−0.05	−0.08
49	22	Reference books (other)	0.09	0.01	0.11	0.07
		Eigenvalue	.9666	.4914	.2614	.2272
		Probability	.1804E-20	.4555E-10	.6562E-06	.5190E-03

Appendix Table 63

Institutional Means on First Four Discriminants

Row	University	Discriminant			
		1	2	3	4
1	Guanajuato	−0.45	1.49	0.82	0.12
2	Guadalajara	−0.66	2.41	1.10	−0.18
3	Estado de México	−0.41	1.33	0.34	−0.48
4	Michoacán	−0.92	1.30	1.40	0.42
5	Nuevo León	−0.48	1.32	1.28	−0.46
6	Monterrey	0.71	1.58	1.19	−0.04
7	San Luis Potosí	−0.58	1.18	1.31	−0.23
8	Sonora	−0.23	0.93	0.88	−0.07
9	Veracruz	−0.43	1.37	0.87	0.20

Appendix Table 64

"Hits" and "Misses" in Institutional Classification of Professors According to Discriminant Weights

	Row	University	Membership According to Discriminant Classification									
			1	2	3	4	5	6	7	8	9	Total
Actual Membership	1	Guanajuato	2	4	6	1	10	1	0	0	5	29
	2	Guadalajara	5	18	3	1	10	0	0	0	3	40
	3	Estado de México	0	1	13	0	2	1	0	0	5	22
	4	Michoacán	1	1	0	6	4	0	5	0	7	24
	5	Nuevo León	0	3	3	2	43	3	6	0	4	64
	6	Monterrey	2	0	1	0	7	39	1	0	3	53
	7	San Luis Potosí	0	1	3	0	19	1	7	2	3	36
	8	Sonora	0	0	2	0	1	2	3	2	3	13
	9	Veracruz	1	1	7	3	15	5	2	0	12	46
		Total	11	29	38	13	111	52	24	4	45	327

Appendix Table 65

Discriminant Analysis: Analysis of Group Centroids*

Row	University	1	2	3	4	5	6	7	8	9
1	Monterrey	--	03	00	03	03	00	00	00	00
2	Sonora	04	--	20	19	18	08	05	05	00
3	San Luis Potosí	01	01	--	47	08	07	05	00	02
4	Nuevo León	02	01	22	--	08	06	03	00	03
5	Veracruz	01	06	13	19	--	17	07	03	05
6	Guanajuato	01	05	13	19	27	--	06	05	06
7	Michoacán	00	00	13	22	19	13	--	03	06
8	Estado de México	02	07	08	06	11	11	03	--	04
9	Guadalajara	00	00	06	11	07	07	00	01	--

*Distance of institutional centroids from each other in terms of percentage of professors at other institutions (off-diagonals) who are further from their own ground centroids than is the centroid (institution) being compared (see explanation in Appendix A).

FURTHER READING

Background reading for a study of the Latin American university should include a perusal of the history of medieval universities. We suggest here only three works: a valuable short history, Charles Homer Haskins, *The Rise of Universities* (Ithaca, N.Y.: Cornell University Press, 1966); a more complete treatment, Nathan Schachner, *Mediaeval Universities* (New York: A. S. Barnes [Perpetua Books], 1962); and the authoritative work, Hastings Rashdall, *Universities of Europe in the Middle Ages*, 3 vols. (London: Oxford University Press, 1936).

For the colonial period in Spanish America, a fine general description of higher education is John Tate Lanning, *Academic Culture in the Spanish Colonies* (London: Oxford University Press, 1940), while an excellent representative institutional history is José Mata Gavidia, *Fundación de la Universidad en Guatemala, 1548-1688* (Guatemala: Editorial Universitaria, 1954). For general reading on the university in the nineteenth and early twentieth centuries, Luis-Alberto Sánchez, *La Universidad Latinoamericana* (Guatemala: Editorial Universitaria, 1949) is perhaps best-known, while the best institutional history is probably Tulio Halperin Donghi, *Historia de la Universidad de Buenos Aires* (Buenos Aires: Editorial Universitaria de Buenos Aires, 1962).

The history of university reform after 1918 is most authoritatively presented in the following three works by Gabriel del Mazo: *La Reforma Universitaria*, Vols. I-III (Buenos Aires: Editorial El Ateneo, 1946); *Reforma Universitaria y Cultura Nacional* (Buenos Aires: Editorial Raigal, 1955); and *Estudiantes y Gobierno Universitario* (Buenos Aires: Librería "El Ateneo" Editorial, second edition, 1955).

Current philosophical analyses of the university abound. The range of viewpoints runs from Sebastián Mayo (a pseudonym), *La Educación Socialista en México: el Asalto a la Universidad Nacional* (Rosario, Argentina: Editorial Bear, 1964), a sympathetic history of the resistance of conservative forces in the universities to the "radical" Cárdenas government, to Humberto Cuenca, La Universidad Revolucionaria (Caracas: Editorial Cultura Contemporanea, 1964), in which it is argued that the university's function is the orientation of the worker-student to the Marxist socialist state.

The university as a cultural center and an instrument for the training of professionals is perhaps best stated in José Ortega y Gasset, Mission of the University (Princeton, N.J.: Princeton University Press, 1944), and a somewhat contradictory emphasis on the importance of research and methodology is best presented in Karl Jaspers, The Idea of the University (Boston: Beacon Press, 1959).

Harold R. W. Benjamin, Higher Education in the American Republics (New York: McGraw-Hill Series in International Development, 1965) is a useful factual source of information in English about the Latin American university. Several good critical analyses of the present structure of the Latin American university are available in English. Most critical and most comprehensive is Rudolf P. Atcon, The Latin American University (Bogotá: Editorial ABC, 1966). A reading of current critical analyses by Latin Americans should include Luis Scherz García, Una Nueva Universidad para América Latina (Maracaibo, Venezuela: Universidad del Zulia, 1965).

The role, particularly the political role, of students in the universities has been the subject of extensive attention. Much bibliographic material is reported in the June 1966 issue of the Comparative Education Review (Vol. X, No. 2), a special issue devoted entirely to student politics. In addition to the writings of such North American scholars as Frank Bonilla, Seymour Martin Lipset, and Kalman Silvert, which emphasize the political role of students, more general analyses of the student culture can be found in the works of Gino Germani and Orlando Albornoz, who write from long personal experience in the Latin American universities.

Bibliographic sources on the Latin American university include the Handbook of Latin American

Studies (Gainesville, Fla.: University of Florida Press, numerous editions); the most recent edition (Vol. XXIX) contains a bibliography of works on the Latin American university annotated by Russell G. Davis and Richard G. King. Volumes XXV and XXVII contain similar bibliographies annotated by Davis. In addition to the Handbook of Latin American Studies, the most useful general bibliography on Latin America is the series edited by Martin Howard Sable, A Guide to Latin American Studies (Los Angeles: University of California Press, 1967). The best bibliography of bibliographies is that of Carl W. Deal, Bibliographic Aids for Collecting Current Latin American Materials, Working Paper No. 22 of the Twelfth Seminar on the Acquisitions of Latin American Library Materials (Washington, D.C.: Pan American Union, 1967).

Additional readings on higher education in Mexico might usefully include the following:

Aguirre Santoscoy, Ramiro. Historia Sociológica de la Educación. México: SEP, 1963.

Alvear Acevedo, Carlos. La Educación y la Ley. México: Jus, 1964.

Attolini, José. Las Finanzas de la Universidad a traves del Tiempo. México: UNAM, 1951.

Bravo Ahuja, Víctor. "La Educación Técnica," in México, 50 Años de Revolución. México: Fondo de Cultura Económica, 1963.

Bravo Ugarte, José. La Educación en México. México: Jus, 1966.

Jimenez Rueda, Julio. "La Universidad Nacional Autónoma de México," in Ensayos Sobre la Universidad de México. México: UNAM, 1951.

Larroyo, Francisco. Historia Comparada de la Educación en México. México: Porrúa, 1964.

Mendieta y Nuñez, Lucio. Historia de la Facultad de Derecho. México: Porrúa, 1956.

Muñoz Ledo, Porfirio. "La Educación Superior," in *México, 50 Años de Revolución*. México: Fondo de Cultura Económica, 1963.

Pani, Alberto. *Una Encuesta Sobre Educación Popular*. México: Dirección de Talleres Gráficos, 1918.

Ruiz Gaitán, Beatriz. *Apuntes para la Historia de la Facultad de Filosofía y Letras*. México: UNAM, 1954.

Siegrist Clamont, Jorgé. *En Defensa de la Autonomía Universitaria; Trayectoría Histórico-Jurídica de la Universidad Mexicana*. México: Universidad Nacional, 1955.

Tamayo, Jorgé. *Breve Reseña Sobre la Escuela Nacioal de Ingeniería*. México: Universidad Nacional, 1958.

Zilli, Juan. *Historia de la Escuela Normal Veracruzana*. México: Citlaltepetl, 1961.

ABOUT THE AUTHORS

RICHARD G. KING is Professor of Educational Research at the University of Alabama in Birmingham. At the time of this study he was a Lecturer in Education and a Research Associate in the Center for Studies in Education and Development of the Harvard Graduate School of Education. His prior experiences included assignment as Associate Director of Admission and Financial Aids and Director of Texts in Harvard College and Assistant Director of the College Entrance Examination Board. He has served as consultant to the Ford Foundation in Colombia, Chile, Mexico and Central America in connection with the Foundation's program of assistance in higher education.

Dr. King, a graduate of Williams College, received his M.A. in Comparative Literature from the Harvard Graduate School of Arts and Sciences and his Ed.D in Educational Measurement from the Harvard Graduate School of Education.

ALFONSO RANGEL GUERRA is the Secretary General of the National Association of Universities and Institutes of Higher Education in Mexico. A former professor and Dean of Humanities at the University of Nuevo León, he has published several books on Mexican literary history and criticism. Prior to the appointment to his present post, he was the Rector of the University of Nuevo León.

DAVID KLINE is a Lecturer and Research Associate at the Center for Studies in Education and Development of the Harvard Graduate School of Education. He also maintains posts as Consultant to the Research Division of the Peace Corps on research priorities, design and evaluation and Consultant to the Citizen Participation Project at Harvard University's Laboratory of Community Development. He has done various reports under Peace Corps contract.

Dr. Kline received his B.A. degree from Bethany Nazarene College, and his M.A. and Ph.D degrees from Michigan State University.

NOEL F. McGINN is an Associate Professor of Education at the Center for Studies in Education and Development at the Harvard Graduate School of Education. Previously, he has served as a Research Associate to the Center for Studies in Education and Development at Harvard University in Venezuela, a program which was attached to the Joint Center for Urban Studies Guayana Project during 1964 and 1965. He has contributed his psychology research papers to such publications as the *Journal of Chronic Diseases*, *Psychological Bulletin* and *Revista Mexicana de Psicologia*.

Dr. McGinn received his B.A. and M.A. degrees from the University of California at Santa Barbara and his Ph.D. from the University of Mighigan.